Contents

Amazon DocumentDB: The Definitive Guide 4

  Part I – Fundamentals of Amazon DocumentDB 8

    Chapter 1: Introduction to Amazon DocumentDB .9

    Chapter 2: Amazon DocumentDB Clusters and Instances 20

    Chapter 3: Pricing and Billing 32

    Chapter 4: Monitoring and Interfaces...................44

  Part II – Architecture and Internal Mechanics 55

    Chapter 5: How Amazon DocumentDB Works 55

    Chapter 6: Storage and Replication 64

    Chapter 7: Endpoints and Connection Models 72

    Chapter 8: Read and Write Consistency Models..84

  Part III – Working with Documents 93

    Chapter 9: Document Database Essentials 93

    Chapter 10: Understanding and Modeling Documents 105

    Chapter 11: CRUD and Querying 116

    Chapter 12: Indexing and Aggregation 127

  Part IV – Getting Started and Deployment.............140

    Chapter 13: Getting Started................................140

    Chapter 14: Quick Start with CloudFormation ...150

  Part V – Compatibility and Extensions 161

    Chapter 15: Elastic Clusters................................161

    Chapter 16: MongoDB Compatibility...................170

Chapter 17: Transactions 181

Chapter 18: API, Operators, and Data Types......192

Part VI – Security and Identity 203

Chapter 19: Security Best Practices...................203

Chapter 20: Identity and Access Management...216

Chapter 21: Auditing and Logging 227

Part VII – Operations and Maintenance 238

Chapter 22: Backup and Restore.........................238

Chapter 23: Maintenance and Patching 250

Chapter 24: Monitoring and Performance Insights
....260

Chapter 25: Managing Resources 270

Part VIII – Migrations and Upgrades 279

Chapter 26: Migrating to DocumentDB 279

Chapter 27: Engine Upgrades 290

Part IX – Real-World Applications and Integrations
....302

Chapter 28: Designing Scalable Document Data
Models 302

Chapter 29: Real-Time Analytics with Amazon
DocumentDB...313

Chapter 30: Serverless Architectures 326

Chapter 31: Microservices with Amazon
DocumentDB...337

Chapter 32: CI/CD Pipelines and Automation.....348

Part X – Enterprise Operations and Strategy 360

Chapter 33: Cost Management and Usage Insights 360

Chapter 34: Auditing and Compliance Use Cases 370

Chapter 35: Hybrid Architectures 380

Chapter 36: AI/ML with DocumentDB 390

Chapter 37: Future Trends and Roadmap 400

Part XI – Tools, Drivers, and Ecosystem 411

Chapter 38: Developing with DocumentDB 411

Chapter 39: Connecting BI Tools 420

Chapter 40: Limits, Quotas, and Troubleshooting 431

Appendices 442

Appendix A: API Reference 442

Appendix B: Useful Links and Further Reading .446

3

Amazon DocumentDB: The Definitive Guide

About the Author

Souren Stepanyan is a cloud solutions architect, technologist, and educator with a passion for serverless technologies and AWS-native architectures. With years of experience designing resilient cloud systems, Souren specializes in building scalable, secure, and high-performing infrastructure for businesses ranging from startups to large enterprises. He is the author of multiple technical books focused on Amazon Web Services, including deep dives into Lambda, S3, IAM, and DynamoDB. When he's not architecting solutions or writing, he enjoys exploring the intersection of AI and cloud, mentoring developers, and simplifying complex concepts for broader audiences.

Who This Book Is For

This book is designed for:

- **Developers** looking to build cloud-native applications with flexible data models
- **Database Administrators (DBAs)** seeking to migrate or manage MongoDB-compatible workloads on AWS
- **Solutions Architects** responsible for designing high-availability, scalable document-based systems
- **DevOps Engineers** interested in automating, monitoring, and optimizing DocumentDB clusters
- **Technical Leaders** evaluating DocumentDB as a managed alternative to MongoDB in production environments

No prior knowledge of Amazon DocumentDB is required, but familiarity with AWS basics, JSON, and NoSQL principles will be helpful.

How to Use This Book

You don't have to read this book cover to cover—though you certainly can.

Each part is modular and designed to help you achieve specific goals:

- **Part I – Fundamentals** introduces core DocumentDB concepts.
- **Part II & III** explore architecture and how to interact with documents effectively.
- **Part IV–VIII** help you deploy, secure, scale, and migrate your data systems.
- **Part IX–XI** dive into real-world use cases, BI tools, CI/CD, AI/ML integration, and troubleshooting.

Use this book as a **reference guide** or an end-to-end tutorial depending on where you are in your cloud journey. Code examples, CLI snippets, AWS Console tips, and architecture best practices are included throughout for hands-on learners.

Introduction

In the era of dynamic, fast-evolving applications, the need for scalable and flexible databases has become a cornerstone of modern architecture. As organizations shift toward microservices, serverless computing, and cloud-native solutions, the role of document databases has grown significantly.

Amazon DocumentDB (with MongoDB compatibility) is AWS's answer to the demand for a managed, scalable document database that delivers MongoDB-like syntax and tooling—without the operational overhead of managing database infrastructure.

This book, **Mastering Amazon DocumentDB**, is your definitive guide to understanding, deploying, and optimizing applications on DocumentDB. Whether you're a developer, solutions architect, or DevOps engineer, this guide is designed to take you from foundational concepts to enterprise-grade implementations.

You'll explore:

- How DocumentDB clusters work under the hood
- Key architectural distinctions between DocumentDB and MongoDB
- Best practices for performance, security, and scalability
- Real-world use cases including analytics, microservices, and hybrid cloud strategies
- End-to-end deployment with automation, CI/CD, and monitoring

Each chapter combines conceptual clarity with hands-on examples, command-line snippets, AWS Console walkthroughs, and architectural tips.

Whether you're migrating from a self-hosted MongoDB environment or designing a greenfield cloud-native application, this guide will empower you to harness the full potential of Amazon DocumentDB and build resilient, performant, and secure systems.

Part I – Fundamentals of Amazon DocumentDB

Chapter 1: Introduction to Amazon DocumentDB

What is Amazon DocumentDB

Amazon DocumentDB (with MongoDB compatibility) is a fully managed, scalable, and highly available document database service designed to run mission-critical applications in the cloud. It is optimized for JSON-like document storage, making it an ideal choice for applications that require flexible schemas, such as content management systems, catalogs, personalization engines, and mobile backends.

Built with MongoDB API compatibility, Amazon DocumentDB enables developers to use the same application code, drivers, and tools they use with MongoDB, significantly easing the migration or integration process. Under the hood, Amazon DocumentDB is designed from the ground up to provide cloud-native scalability, fault tolerance, and high durability, leveraging AWS infrastructure strengths.

Some of the core use cases for Amazon DocumentDB include:

- Content management systems

- User profile management

- Real-time analytics

- IoT applications

- Catalog and inventory systems

Let's explore Amazon DocumentDB's foundational elements and its architectural innovations that differentiate it from self-managed MongoDB databases.

Core Features and Architecture

Amazon DocumentDB introduces several features that provide performance, scalability, and management benefits, making it a robust database option for modern application development.

Fully Managed Infrastructure

Amazon DocumentDB removes the burden of infrastructure management, allowing developers and DBAs to focus on building applications. Key management tasks such as provisioning hardware, patching software, configuring backups, and handling failover are automated.

Benefits include:

- No server maintenance

- Automatic software patching

- Seamless version upgrades

- Elastic compute and storage scaling

MongoDB API Compatibility

Amazon DocumentDB supports MongoDB APIs and drivers, specifically versions 3.6, 4.0, and 5.0. This allows developers to:

- Use existing MongoDB drivers

- Reuse current code and queries

- Simplify migration from self-hosted MongoDB

While compatibility is high, there are certain functional differences, especially with advanced MongoDB features such as sharding and some specific operators. Developers should always refer to the functional differences documentation when planning migrations.

Document Model and Flexible Schema

Amazon DocumentDB uses a JSON-like document model to store data, offering flexibility and rich indexing options.

- Documents are stored in BSON format (binary JSON)

- Fields in documents can contain arrays and nested documents

- No fixed schema: fields can vary between documents in a collection

This model is particularly suited to applications with dynamic data models or semi-structured data.

Separation of Compute and Storage

A core architectural difference between Amazon DocumentDB and traditional MongoDB is the **separation of compute and storage**, providing cloud-native scalability and high availability.

Cluster Components:

- **Primary Instance:** Handles all write operations and can serve reads

- **Replica Instances (up to 15):** Read-only nodes that share storage with the primary

- **Cluster Volume:** A virtual volume that stores six copies of data across three Availability Zones (AZs)

Advantages of this separation:

- Read replicas can be provisioned or removed without affecting data availability

- All nodes share the same underlying storage, so replicas do not require additional synchronization

- Storage scales automatically in 10 GB increments up to 128 TiB

High Availability and Automatic Failover

Amazon DocumentDB provides enterprise-grade reliability through its replication and failover capabilities.

Availability features include:

- Data replicated six ways across three AZs

- Automatic failover to a replica instance in case the primary fails

- Continuous monitoring and automatic instance restarts

If no replicas are provisioned, Amazon DocumentDB attempts to create a new primary instance in the event of a failure. These mechanisms ensure minimal downtime and high service continuity.

Performance and Scalability

Amazon DocumentDB is built for performance at scale:

- **Read Scaling:** Up to 15 read replicas per cluster

- **Elastic Compute:** Resize instance classes with minimal downtime

- **I/O Optimization:** Choose between standard and I/O-optimized storage configurations

- **Storage Auto-Scaling:** Automatic growth based on usage, up to 128 TiB

Amazon DocumentDB's distributed storage system is optimized for low-latency reads and writes with minimal replica lag, even under high throughput workloads.

Security and Compliance

Security is deeply integrated into Amazon DocumentDB's design, offering features such as:

- **Encryption at Rest:** Using AWS Key Management Service (KMS)

- **Encryption in Transit:** TLS support for secure connections

- **Network Isolation:** Using Amazon VPC

- **Authentication and Authorization:** Integration with AWS IAM, support for role-based access control (RBAC)

- **Audit Logging:** Available for compliance tracking

Amazon DocumentDB is compliant with standards including FedRAMP, SOC, and HIPAA, making it suitable for regulated industries.

Backup and Restore

Amazon DocumentDB includes automated backup and restore capabilities for disaster recovery and operational resilience:

- **Point-in-Time Recovery:** Restore to any second within the retention window (up to 35 days)

- **Automatic Backups:** Continuous and incremental, with no performance impact

- **Manual Snapshots:** Create and retain snapshots manually for long-term storage or auditing

- **Restore to New Cluster:** Create a clone from a snapshot for testing or migration

All backups are stored in Amazon S3, ensuring high durability and availability.

Developer Interfaces and Tooling

Amazon DocumentDB supports multiple access methods for development and management:

- **AWS Management Console:** Web UI for provisioning and monitoring

- **AWS CLI and SDKs:** Automate operations and integrate into DevOps workflows

- **MongoDB Drivers:** Use existing libraries for Python, Java, Node.js, etc.

- **TLS and Replica Set Modes:** Connect securely and efficiently

Additionally, tools like **mongodump**, **mongorestore**, **mongoimport**, and **mongoexport** can be used for data migration and manipulation.

Monitoring and Diagnostics

Amazon DocumentDB integrates with Amazon CloudWatch and AWS CloudTrail for operational visibility:

- **Performance Metrics:** Monitor CPU, memory, replica lag, IOPS, and more

- **Logs:** Export audit and profiler logs for analysis

- **Alarms:** Set CloudWatch alarms for automated alerting

- **Performance Insights:** Deep-dive into query behavior and bottlenecks

Monitoring is essential for tuning queries, scaling decisions, and identifying anomalous behavior.

Summary of Core Architecture Components

Component	Description
Cluster	A logical container for instances and shared storage
Primary Instance	Handles writes and read operations
Replicas	Support horizontal read scaling (up to 15)
Cluster Volume	Cloud-native storage layer, replicated across 3 AZs
Endpoints	Cluster, reader, and instance-specific connection addresses
TLS Support	Ensures data is encrypted in transit
IAM and RBAC	Control authentication and fine-grained access
Backups	Continuous, automated, and incremental

Example: Connecting to Amazon DocumentDB

To connect programmatically using the MongoDB shell with TLS and replica set mode:

```
mongo "mongodb://myUser:myPassword@sample-cluster.cluster-abcdefghijkl.us-west-
```

2.docdb.amazonaws.com:27017/?replicaSet=rs0&tls=true
&tlsCAFile=rds-combined-ca-bundle.pem"

This ensures:

- Encrypted connection

- Cluster-wide failover support

- Read preference options via replicaSet mode

Best Practices Snapshot

- **Use cluster endpoints** in replica set mode for most applications

- **Distribute read workloads** using replicas and read preference settings

- **Enable automatic backups** and understand retention windows

- **Monitor metrics** regularly to identify and tune performance bottlenecks

- **Use IAM policies** for granular security management

Final Thoughts

Amazon DocumentDB offers a modern, cloud-optimized, fully managed document database service for developers building scalable, high-performance applications. By combining the flexibility of the document model with AWS's operational excellence, DocumentDB provides a powerful alternative to self-managed MongoDB.

In the following chapters, we will dive deeper into cluster management, document operations, monitoring, security, performance optimization, and migration strategies to help you become proficient in Amazon DocumentDB development and administration.

Chapter 2: Amazon DocumentDB Clusters and Instances

Clusters, Instances, Regions, and AZs

Amazon DocumentDB (with MongoDB compatibility) provides a cloud-native, scalable, and managed database service designed for JSON document storage. At the core of its architecture are **clusters and instances**, the fundamental building blocks that manage your data and compute resources. This chapter explores how Amazon DocumentDB clusters are structured, the role of instances, how these components are deployed across AWS Regions and Availability Zones (AZs), and how this distributed architecture enhances durability, availability, and fault tolerance.

Understanding Amazon DocumentDB Clusters

An **Amazon DocumentDB cluster** is the primary container for your database resources. Each cluster is composed of:

- A **cluster volume**, which stores your data

- One or more **instances**, which provide the compute and memory resources for your applications

Amazon DocumentDB separates **compute and storage**, allowing independent scaling and improving overall system flexibility. This separation is pivotal to understanding how Amazon DocumentDB achieves high availability, durability, and performance.

Cluster Volume

- Each cluster has a **single virtual storage volume** that is automatically replicated across three Availability Zones.

- It stores up to **128 TiB** of data and grows automatically in increments of **10 GiB** as needed.

- Data is replicated **six times** for redundancy: two copies in each of three AZs.

This design enables **high availability** and **fault tolerance** by ensuring that even if an entire AZ becomes unavailable, the cluster continues to operate.

Cluster Roles

Each Amazon DocumentDB cluster includes:

- **One primary instance**: Handles both read and write operations.

- **Up to 15 replica instances**: Handle **read-only** queries and serve as failover targets in case of primary instance failure.

This architecture ensures that the **write load is centralized**, simplifying consistency and durability, while the **read load is distributed**, enhancing performance and scalability.

Amazon DocumentDB Instances

An **instance** is an isolated compute resource in a DocumentDB cluster. Each instance provides CPU, RAM, and networking capability for database operations. These instances come in various **classes**, tailored to meet specific performance and cost requirements.

Types of Instances

1. **Primary Instance**

    - Performs all **write operations**.

    - Serves **read traffic** as well.

    - There is **only one primary instance** per cluster.

2. **Replica Instances**

    - Perform **read operations only**.

    - Up to **15 replicas** can be added.

    - Automatically promoted in case the primary fails.

Replica instances provide **horizontal read scaling** and play a critical role in **high availability** and **automatic failover**.

Instance Classes

Amazon DocumentDB supports several instance classes optimized for memory, I/O, or general-purpose workloads. For example:

- **Memory optimized**: db.r6g, db.r5

- **Burstable performance**: db.t3, db.t4g

- **NVMe-backed options** for enhanced performance

Instances can be resized to a different class with minimal downtime, enabling flexibility to respond to workload changes.

Creating and Managing Instances

- Instances are launched into a cluster via the **AWS Console**, **CLI**, or **SDKs**.

- Compute capacity can be **scaled vertically** by changing the instance class.

- Replica instances can be **added or removed dynamically** to match read demands.

Amazon DocumentDB supports up to **16 total instances** per cluster, including the primary.

Regions and Availability Zones (AZs)

Amazon DocumentDB is built on top of AWS infrastructure and uses AWS's global Regions and AZs to achieve **geographic distribution**, **resilience**, and **low latency**.

What Is an AWS Region?

A **Region** is a physical location in the world where AWS has multiple data centers. Each Region operates independently and is **geographically isolated**.

Amazon DocumentDB is available in most commercial and government Regions. Examples include:

- **us-east-1 (N. Virginia)**

- **eu-west-1 (Ireland)**

- **ap-southeast-1 (Singapore)**

- **us-gov-west-1 (AWS GovCloud)**

Availability Zones

Each Region contains **multiple Availability Zones (AZs)** — distinct locations with independent power, networking, and connectivity.

- **AZs are designed for fault isolation**: a failure in one AZ does not impact others.

- Amazon DocumentDB uses AZs to:

  - Replicate storage six ways across **three AZs**

  - Distribute **compute instances** for fault tolerance

This means your cluster remains available even if one AZ is completely offline.

Cluster Storage and Data Durability

One of the most notable architectural innovations in Amazon DocumentDB is its **cloud-native storage layer**:

- Every **write** operation is **committed to the cluster volume**, which is then **replicated across AZs**.

- This approach avoids the need to replicate to each instance manually.

- **Instance restarts** arc faot bccouoc tho **databaco cache** is separate and can survive restarts.

Data durability and high availability are inherent, not dependent on the number of instances.

Multi-AZ Compute Deployment and Failover

Amazon DocumentDB supports **multi-AZ deployments** for both storage and compute.

Compute Availability

- You can deploy **replica instances across multiple AZs**.

- In case the **primary instance fails**, Amazon DocumentDB automatically:

    ○ Promotes the **most up-to-date replica** to become the new primary.

    ○ Redirects the **cluster endpoint** to the new primary instance.

Storage Redundancy

- Storage is **quorum-based and self-healing**.

- If any copy becomes corrupt or unavailable, it is automatically rebuilt from healthy replicas.

Read Scaling and Performance

To handle high read throughput:

- Add **read replicas** across AZs.

- Use the **reader endpoint**, which load balances connections to available replicas.

- Alternatively, connect using **replica set mode** and specify secondaryPreferred to optimize reads.

Amazon DocumentDB read replicas are:

- **Eventually consistent**

- Typically have **<100ms lag**

- Serve **ordered and consistent reads**

Instance Placement Strategy

Best practices for deploying instances across AZs:

- **Minimum two AZs** for production environments.

- Distribute **replica instances evenly** across AZs.

- Use **reader endpoint** or **replica set mode** for efficient read routing.

- Avoid assuming an instance's role (primary or replica) based on its endpoint — use cluster endpoint or replica set mode for reliability.

Tips for Managing Clusters and Instances

💡 **TIP**: Always monitor cluster health with Amazon CloudWatch. Set alarms for metrics like CPUUtilization, FreeableMemory, and ReplicationLag.

💡 **TIP**: Use **Amazon CloudTrail** to track API-level changes to clusters and instances.

💡 **TIP**: Enable **TLS** for in-transit encryption and use **AWS KMS** for encrypting data at rest.

Cluster Lifecycle

The lifecycle of a cluster and its instances involves several stages:

1. **Creation**

   ○ Initiated via AWS Console or CLI

   ○ Define instance types, storage mode (standard vs. I/O-optimized), and encryption options

2. **Operation**

   ○ Ongoing reads/writes, backups, monitoring

   ○ Dynamic instance scaling and storage auto-growth

3. **Scaling**

   ○ Add or remove instances based on load

   ○ Vertically scale instance class

4. **Failover**

   ○ Automatic promotion of replicas

   ○ Endpoint redirection handled seamlessly

5. **Deletion**

   ○ Remove all instances

   ○ Delete cluster (manual snapshots can be retained)

Supported Regions and Instance Classes

Not all instance classes are available in every Region. Amazon provides a detailed matrix of support across:

- **Instance types**: r6gd, r6g, r5, r4, t4g, t3

- **Regions**: Full coverage across North America, Europe, Asia-Pacific, GovCloud, and China

Always verify compatibility based on your Region before deploying.

Cost Considerations

Pricing varies by:

- **Instance class**

- **Storage used** (GB-months)

- **I/O operations**

- **Data transfer**

🔍 Use the AWS Pricing Calculator to estimate DocumentDB costs.

Summary

Amazon DocumentDB clusters and instances provide a resilient, highly available architecture for document database workloads. The core concepts include:

- Clusters with **shared, auto-replicated storage**

- Separation of **compute and storage**

- Up to **16 instances per cluster**, with **read replicas** for scaling

- **Automatic failover, AZ-aware deployments**, and **auto-healing storage**

- **Regional availability** with broad global support

This distributed architecture allows developers and database administrators to build robust, scalable applications without worrying about the underlying infrastructure complexity. Clusters can adapt dynamically to changing workloads, and best practices in AZ distribution and failover help ensure continuous availability.

Chapter 3: Pricing and Billing

Pricing Structure

Amazon DocumentDB offers a flexible, pay-as-you-go pricing model designed to accommodate a wide variety of use cases and organizational scales. By decoupling compute, storage, and I/O, DocumentDB allows you to scale each independently and only pay for what you consume. This approach is particularly beneficial for dynamic workloads or applications with fluctuating demands.

At a high level, Amazon DocumentDB's pricing comprises the following key components:

- **Instance Hours**

- **I/O Requests**

- **Backup Storage**

- **Data Transfer**

Let's explore each of these elements in detail.

Instance Hours

Instance hours are billed on a per-second basis with a minimum charge of 10 minutes. Each instance you provision incurs charges depending on its **instance class** and **operating time**.

- For example, if you use a db.r5.large instance, you are billed based on the hourly rate for that instance class, regardless of whether it's the primary or a replica.

- Charges accrue whether the instance is idle or actively processing queries.

- Billing stops only when the instance is terminated.

This billing model allows for fine-grained cost control and aligns well with workloads that require elasticity, such as development, testing, and analytics tasks.

I/O Requests

I/O requests are operations that interact with the underlying storage layer. Amazon DocumentDB storage is decoupled from compute and automatically replicated across six copies in three Availability Zones for high durability and availability.

- You are charged per million I/O requests each month.

- Operations such as reads, writes, and background processes like index maintenance generate I/O requests.

Use cases with high write throughput or frequent data manipulation will typically see more significant I/O charges.

Backup Storage

Amazon DocumentDB provides **automated backups** and supports **manual snapshots**, both of which incur backup storage costs.

- **Automated backups** are incremental and continuous, minimizing their impact on performance and reducing unnecessary data duplication.

- Backup storage is billed per GiB per month.

- You are only charged for backup storage beyond the allocated free backup retention space provided by the primary storage volume.

- Increasing the backup retention period or creating more manual snapshots increases the total backup storage used, and therefore the cost.

It's important to note that **deleting unused snapshots** and reducing the backup retention period can directly lower backup-related costs.

Data Transfer

Data transfer charges apply when data moves:

- **In and out of your Amazon DocumentDB instance from/to the internet**

- **Between AWS Regions**

There is no additional charge for data transferred **within the same AWS Region**, such as between Amazon

DocumentDB and Amazon EC2 in the same Availability Zone.

In addition, AWS provides **1 GB per month** of free data transfer out to the internet as part of its Free Tier across all services.

Free Trial

Amazon DocumentDB offers a **free trial** designed to help new users get familiar with the platform without incurring costs. This is ideal for developers evaluating the service or performing short-term proofs of concept.

The free trial includes:

- **750 instance hours** per month of usage with a db.t3.medium instance

- **30 million I/O requests**

- **5 GB of storage**

- **5 GB of backup storage**

The free trial is available for **one month** from the time you create your first DocumentDB cluster. During this period:

- If your usage stays within these thresholds, you won't be charged.

- If your usage exceeds the thresholds, standard DocumentDB pricing applies for the excess usage.

Important Notes:

- The free trial **does not renew**.

- After one month, all usage is billed at standard rates.

- You can track your usage using the AWS Management Console and set up billing alarms to avoid unexpected charges.

The free trial is especially beneficial for:

- Initial exploration of DocumentDB features

- Creating test or sandbox environments

- Developing and validating applications before full deployment

Billable Resources

Understanding which resources are billable is essential for managing your DocumentDB costs effectively. Amazon DocumentDB bills for the following:

1. Instances

Each instance in your cluster — whether it's the primary or a replica — is a billable resource.

- Charged by the instance class and runtime duration

- Includes all associated compute and memory resources

- Does not vary by region, although prices may differ by location

You can have up to **16 instances per cluster** (1 primary + 15 replicas), each contributing to your monthly charges.

2. I/O Operations

All operations that involve the storage layer are counted as billable I/O:

- Insert, update, and delete operations

- Index creation and maintenance

- Query execution that involves disk reads

Even system processes like background compactions and data cleanups contribute to I/O request count.

Best Practices to Reduce I/O Charges:

- Use efficient queries and indexes

- Avoid unnecessary write operations

- Monitor I/O patterns using CloudWatch metrics

3. Storage

DocumentDB storage includes:

- Active database storage (automatically scaled in 10 GB increments)

- Backup storage (for snapshots and point-in-time recovery)

- Logs and metadata

Storage charges apply only to the data you use, with no need for manual provisioning. The maximum cluster volume can scale up to **128 TiB**, though charges are based only on allocated and used space.

4. Backup Retention

The backup retention policy allows up to **35 days** of point-in-time recovery:

- Backups are stored in Amazon S3, which provides 11 9's durability

- Retaining more historical data increases costs

- Manual snapshots are also billable as long as they are retained

You can manage backup lifecycle using automated tools or manually through the AWS Console or CLI.

5. Snapshots

Snapshots are billed separately from automated backups:

- Manual snapshots are retained until deleted, regardless of your backup retention settings

- Copying a snapshot to another Region incurs additional charges for both storage and inter-region data transfer

Snapshots are commonly used for:

- Environment cloning

- Backup validation

- Cross-Region disaster recovery

6. Data Transfer

Cross-region or external data transfers are billable. Charges are as follows:

- **Between AWS Regions**: Billed per GB

- **To the internet**: Billed per GB

- **Within the same region**: Typically free (exceptions may apply for specialized services)

To optimize data transfer costs:

- Deploy application and database resources in the same region

- Use VPC peering or AWS PrivateLink where possible

7. Monitoring and Logging

Monitoring services like **Amazon CloudWatch** and **AWS CloudTrail** are integral to managing DocumentDB performance, and they have their own pricing models.

- **CloudWatch metrics**: Basic monitoring is free; detailed metrics are charged per metric

- **CloudTrail**: Logs DocumentDB API calls for auditing and compliance; pricing depends on the volume and retention

Other features such as **Performance Insights** offer deeper diagnostics and are also billable beyond the free tier.

8. Encryption Key Usage (KMS)

If you use AWS Key Management Service (KMS) for encryption, you may incur additional charges for:

- **Creating and storing KMS keys**

- **Encrypting/decrypting operations**

These are typically minor but can accumulate in high-throughput environments.

9. Change Streams

DocumentDB supports **change streams**, which allow you to listen to real-time changes in your data. These streams are useful for:

- Event-driven applications

- Integrating with AWS Lambda

- Real-time analytics

Change streams have associated I/O costs and can also increase network usage if integrated with external systems like OpenSearch or S3.

10. AWS DMS (Database Migration Service)

For users migrating to DocumentDB, AWS DMS may be used:

- DMS charges for replication instances, storage, and data transfer

- Enables minimal-downtime migrations

- Also useful for ongoing data replication or hybrid deployments

11. Elastic Clusters (Optional)

If using **Amazon DocumentDB elastic clusters**, there are separate billing considerations:

- Shard count and compute capacity per shard

- Storage and I/O per shard

- Cluster management overhead

Elastic clusters are designed for large-scale workloads and offer granular control over cost and performance.

Summary and Optimization Tips

To effectively manage and optimize your Amazon DocumentDB billing:

- **Monitor usage regularly** using AWS Cost Explorer and CloudWatch

- **Choose the appropriate instance class** based on workload requirements

- **Use auto-scaling** judiciously to manage spikes in demand

- **Enable alerts** for I/O usage, storage thresholds, and data transfer

- **Regularly clean up** old snapshots, unused indexes, and redundant replicas

- **Align resources** with your application lifecycle stages — for example, using t3.medium during development and r6g.large in production

By understanding and proactively managing these billable components, organizations can leverage the full power of Amazon DocumentDB without incurring unexpected costs.

Chapter 4: Monitoring and Interfaces

CloudWatch, AWS CLI, Console, MongoDB Drivers

Overview

Effective monitoring and flexible interfaces are essential components of managing any production-grade database system. In Amazon DocumentDB (with MongoDB compatibility), AWS provides a comprehensive suite of tools for tracking performance, diagnosing issues, and interacting with your database. These tools ensure observability, enable automated and manual operations, and maintain the health and efficiency of your clusters and instances.

This chapter covers the available monitoring options in Amazon DocumentDB—primarily through **Amazon CloudWatch**, **AWS CLI**, and the **AWS Management Console**—and explores how to interact programmatically using **MongoDB drivers**.

Monitoring Amazon DocumentDB

Amazon DocumentDB offers integrated monitoring to help developers and operations teams understand the health, performance, and resource utilization of their database deployments.

Monitoring tools include:

- **Amazon CloudWatch** for real-time metrics and alarms

- **Event subscriptions** for proactive alerts

- **Performance Insights** (in select regions) for deeper query analysis

- **AWS CLI tools** for automation and scripting

Key Monitoring Concepts

Amazon DocumentDB clusters and instances generate a variety of metrics that reflect performance, utilization, and health. These include:

- CPU and memory usage

- Disk I/O and latency

- Connection counts

- Replica lag

- Throttling and resource constraints

All metrics are made available through **CloudWatch**, allowing for historical analysis, dashboard creation, and automated alerting.

Amazon CloudWatch Integration

Amazon CloudWatch is a central service used to collect and track metrics, collect and monitor log files, and set alarms. Amazon DocumentDB integrates natively with CloudWatch to expose relevant database metrics.

Common Metrics

Some of the most useful CloudWatch metrics for DocumentDB include:

- CPUUtilization: Percentage of compute resource usage

- DatabaseConnections: Active client connections

- FreeableMemory: Amount of unused memory

- ReadIOPS and WriteIOPS: I/O operations per second

- ReplicaLag: Time delay between the primary and replica instances

- VolumeBytesUsed: Storage usage

- LowMemThrottleQueueDepth: Number of operations throttled due to low memory

Setting Alarms

You can create alarms on any metric to get notified when thresholds are breached. For example:

If CPUUtilization > 80% for 5 minutes → send SNS notification

This helps detect performance degradation or over-utilization early, allowing teams to take action before users are affected.

CloudWatch Dashboards

You can use CloudWatch dashboards to visualize and monitor multiple metrics from different instances or clusters in one consolidated view.

CloudWatch Logs

Amazon DocumentDB also supports logging through **CloudTrail** and **Profiler logs** which can be routed to CloudWatch Logs for long-term storage and analysis.

Event Subscriptions

Amazon DocumentDB provides an event notification system that allows you to receive alerts when specific changes or issues occur. Event categories include:

- Cluster and instance availability

- Backup and restore operations

- Failover events

- Maintenance window notifications

- Parameter group modifications

Subscription Example

You can subscribe to receive notifications through **Amazon SNS (Simple Notification Service)**. This allows for real-time alerts via email, SMS, or Lambda invocation.

Using the AWS Management Console

The AWS Management Console provides a graphical interface for managing DocumentDB clusters and instances. It is ideal for users who prefer visual management over scripting or API usage.

Console Features

- Launching and modifying clusters and instances

- Monitoring metrics (with integrated CloudWatch graphs)

- Performing backups and restores

- Managing security and access (VPC, IAM, and encryption settings)

- Accessing cluster endpoints and connection strings

- Viewing and exporting logs and snapshots

Benefits of Using the Console

- No coding required

- Visual graphs for quick status assessment

- Easy access to configuration settings

- One-click actions for common tasks (e.g., add replica, failover test, snapshot creation)

Monitoring with the AWS CLI

The AWS Command Line Interface (CLI) enables automation and scripting of all operations supported in the Amazon DocumentDB service.

Installing the AWS CLI

To begin, install the CLI from the AWS CLI documentation, then configure it using:

```
aws configure
```

You'll be prompted to enter:

- AWS Access Key ID

- AWS Secret Access Key

- Default Region

- Output Format (e.g., JSON)

Common AWS CLI Commands

List clusters:

```
aws docdb describe-db-clusters
```

List instances in a cluster:

```
aws docdb describe-db-instances --db-cluster-identifier
my-docdb-cluster
```

Monitor CPU utilization with CloudWatch:

```
aws cloudwatch get-metric-statistics \
  --metric-name CPUUtilization \
  --start-time 2025-03-26T00:00:00Z \
  --end-time 2025-03-27T00:00:00Z \
  --period 3600 \
  --namespace AWS/DocDB \
  --statistics Average \
  --dimensions Name=DBInstanceIdentifier,Value=my-
docdb-instance
```

Trigger a manual failover:

```
aws docdb failover-db-cluster --db-cluster-identifier my-
docdb-cluster
```

Automation Use Cases

- Create daily snapshots via scheduled scripts

- Scale read replicas during high-traffic events

- Monitor and alert on resource metrics

- Rotate cluster credentials securely

Connecting with MongoDB Drivers

Amazon DocumentDB is compatible with MongoDB drivers, enabling seamless integration with existing MongoDB applications. You can use the same drivers, tools, and libraries that work with MongoDB 3.6, 4.0, and 5.0.

Recommended Drivers

- Node.js MongoDB Driver

- Python PyMongo

- Java MongoDB Java Driver

- Go Driver

- .NET Driver

Connection String Example

```
mongodb://username:password@sample-cluster.cluster-
123456789012.us-east-
1.docdb.amazonaws.com:27017/?replicaSet=rs0
```

You can also use reader endpoints for read-scaling:

```
mongodb://username:password@sample-cluster.cluster-
ro-123456789012.us-east-
1.docdb.amazonaws.com:27017
```

TLS Considerations

Amazon DocumentDB requires or strongly recommends connecting over TLS. Most drivers support TLS by default, but some require the path to the Amazon root CA certificate:

```
--ssl \
--sslCAFile rds-combined-ca-bundle.pem
```

Read Preference Options

MongoDB drivers support specifying **read preferences**, which define how read requests are routed:

- primary – Strong consistency

- primaryPreferred – Strong consistency when possible, but fallback to replicas

- secondary – Eventual consistency, good for analytics

- secondaryPreferred – Prefer replicas, but fallback to primary

- nearest – Low latency, no consistency guarantees

Replica Set Mode

DocumentDB clusters emulate replica sets. When connecting in replica set mode (?replicaSet=rs0), the driver is aware of multiple instances and can route read requests intelligently.

Best Practices

- **Use CloudWatch Alarms** to detect anomalies early and automate response actions (e.g., scale up, trigger Lambda).

- **Connect in replica set mode** to take advantage of failover and read scaling.

- **Distribute read workload** using readPreference=secondaryPreferred.

- **Avoid direct connections to instance endpoints** in production to ensure resilience.

- **Secure connections with TLS** and rotate credentials using Secrets Manager.

- **Use the AWS CLI** for automation in DevOps workflows and infrastructure as code (IaC).

- **Visualize key metrics** in CloudWatch dashboards for live monitoring.

Summary

Amazon DocumentDB provides rich monitoring and interface capabilities designed for observability, resilience, and developer convenience. With CloudWatch for detailed metrics, AWS CLI for scripting and automation, a user-friendly Console for visual management, and MongoDB driver compatibility for application integration, DocumentDB ensures that both DevOps and development teams can efficiently manage their databases.

These tools together create a highly manageable and robust environment for modern document-based applications, whether you're operating small microservices or scaling enterprise-level data systems.

Part II – Architecture and Internal Mechanics

Chapter 5: How Amazon DocumentDB Works

Amazon DocumentDB is designed with cloud-native architecture principles that prioritize scalability, reliability, and fault tolerance. At the heart of its operation are three key elements: **cluster volumes, instance roles**, and the **write and read paths**. Understanding how these components interact helps developers and architects make better decisions about designing, scaling, and operating their DocumentDB workloads.

Cluster Volumes

Amazon DocumentDB clusters are powered by a decoupled architecture that separates compute and storage. This approach offers several operational advantages and is centered around the concept of **cluster volumes**.

What is a Cluster Volume?

A **cluster volume** in Amazon DocumentDB is a virtualized, cloud-native storage layer that stores your data. It is shared by all instances in a cluster—both primary and replicas—and spans multiple Availability Zones (AZs) for high availability and durability.

Key characteristics of cluster volumes include:

- **Multi-AZ replication**: Six copies of your data are maintained across three Availability Zones.

- **Automatic scaling**: The volume automatically grows in 10 GB increments up to **128 TiB**.

- **Durability**: Designed for 99.999999999% durability using Amazon's distributed storage technology.

- **Shared access**: All instances (primary and replicas) in the cluster interact with a single, centralized volume.

Benefits of Cluster Volumes

- **Decoupled compute and storage** allows for independent scaling of resources.

- **Fast failovers** due to no need for data replication between instances.

- **Reduced replica lag**, typically in the low milliseconds, as all instances share the same underlying storage.

Tip: Understanding Storage Costs

Amazon DocumentDB charges for **actual data used**, not provisioned storage. For versions 4.0 and above, deleting data (collections, indexes) frees space and reduces costs. For version 3.6, you may need to recreate the cluster to reset the storage high-water mark.

Instance Roles

Each Amazon DocumentDB cluster consists of up to **16 instances**, which play specific roles:

Primary Instance

- **Handles all writes and updates**

- Supports reads as well

- Acts as the **cluster leader** in routing data operations

- There is only **one primary instance** per cluster at any time

Replica Instances

- Support **read-only operations**

- Up to **15 replicas** can be configured in a cluster

- Serve read traffic to reduce load on the primary

- Automatically promoted to **primary** in the event of a failover

Instance Role Summary

Role	Read Support	Write Support	Failover Eligible	Quantity Limit

Primary	Yes	Yes	Not applicable	1
Replica	Yes	No	Yes	Up to 15

Tip: Replica Placement

To maximize availability, distribute replica instances across **multiple Availability Zones**. This setup allows for seamless failovers without losing read capacity.

Write and Read Paths

Amazon DocumentDB's design optimizes both **write durability** and **read scalability** through clearly defined data paths.

Write Path

The write path in Amazon DocumentDB ensures high durability and availability:

1. **Application writes to the cluster endpoint** (which resolves to the primary instance).

2. The **primary instance** validates and applies the write operation.

3. The **write is persisted** to the cluster volume.

4. A **write acknowledgment** is only sent after the majority of storage nodes have durably stored the data.

Write Characteristics

- Atomic at the **document level**

- Write concern is always effectively { w:3, j:true }—
  cannot be modified

- Highly durable—even single-instance clusters offer
  full write durability

Important Notes

- Writes to replicas or the reader endpoint **fail with
  errors**

- DocumentDB **ignores** wtimeout **and other write
  concern configurations**

Read Path

The read path in Amazon DocumentDB supports both
strong and **eventual consistency**, depending on the
chosen read preference.

Read from Primary (Strong Consistency)

- Routed through the **cluster endpoint**

- Reads return the most recent acknowledged writes

- Suitable for applications needing **read-after-write**
  consistency

Read from Replicas (Eventual Consistency)

- Routed through the **reader endpoint** or using **read preferences**

- Reads may lag behind primary by **<100 ms**

- Ideal for **analytics and read-heavy workloads**

Read Preferences

DocumentDB supports standard MongoDB read preferences when connected in **replica set mode**:

- primary: Always read from the primary

- primaryPreferred: Read from primary if available, else a replica

- secondary: Always read from a replica

- secondaryPreferred: Prefer replica, fallback to primary

- nearest: Read from the instance with the lowest network latency

Example: Connecting in replica set mode

mongodb://username:password@sample-cluster.cluster-xyz.us-east-1.docdb.amazonaws.com:27017/?replicaSet=rs0

Comparison of Read Modes

Mode	Use Case	Consistency	Fallback Behavior
primary	Transactional systems	Strong	Errors on failover
primaryPreferred	Mixed workloads	Strong (most cases)	Switch to eventual
secondary	Analytics	Eventual	Errors if no replica
secondaryPreferred	Balanced performance	Eventual	Reads from primary
nearest	Latency-sensitive applications	Eventual	Closest instance

Replica Set Mode

Amazon DocumentDB **emulates MongoDB replica sets**, even though it doesn't rely on multiple data replicas for durability.

- The **replica set name is always** rs0

- Allows MongoDB drivers to manage failovers and load balancing

- Required for **read preference**, **read concern**, and **write concern** settings to function

Failover Behavior

Amazon DocumentDB automates failovers to ensure high availability:

- When a **primary instance fails**, a **replica is promoted** to primary.

- The **cluster endpoint** updates DNS to point to the new primary.

- Failovers usually complete in **under 30 seconds**.

- If **no replicas exist**, a new primary is automatically created (if capacity allows).

Tip: Monitor for Failovers

Use Amazon CloudWatch metrics like:

- DatabaseConnections

- ReplicaLag

- FailoverEvents

These help track cluster health and readiness for failover scenarios.

Summary

Amazon DocumentDB's architecture, built on the principles of decoupled compute and storage, provides robust support for mission-critical applications with demanding availability, consistency, and performance requirements. Understanding **cluster volumes**, the roles of **primary and**

replica instances, and the **read/write data paths** empowers developers to:

- Optimize cluster configuration

- Balance read scalability and write consistency

- Architect resilient applications with minimal downtime

Chapter 6: Storage and Replication

SSD-backed Storage

Amazon DocumentDB utilizes a cloud-native, SSD-backed storage architecture that is purpose-built for high performance, scalability, and durability. Unlike traditional database systems that couple compute and storage resources tightly, Amazon DocumentDB decouples them, allowing the system to scale each independently for efficiency and cost-effectiveness.

Architecture Overview

- **Cluster Volume**: The core storage unit in Amazon DocumentDB is the *cluster volume*, a virtualized volume that spans across three AWS Availability Zones (AZs).

- **SSD Utilization**: The underlying infrastructure uses solid-state drives (SSDs) to deliver low-latency, high-throughput performance, ideal for document-based workloads with frequent reads and writes.

- **Automatic Growth**: The cluster volume automatically grows in 10 GB increments as needed, with a maximum size of **128 TiB**, eliminating the need for manual storage provisioning.

Key Benefits

- **High IOPS and Low Latency**: SSDs provide the necessary input/output operations per second

(IOPS) required for read- and write-intensive applications.

- **Cost Efficiency**: You are billed only for the actual data stored, not the allocated volume, making storage costs predictable and optimized.

- **Resilience and Redundancy**: Each piece of data is replicated across multiple physical locations (AZs), mitigating risks from hardware failures.

Dynamic Storage Management

Starting from **Amazon DocumentDB version 4.0**, the platform introduces automatic space reclamation. This means that when collections, indexes, or entire databases are dropped, the allocated storage is reduced accordingly. This contrasts with version 3.6, where storage usage follows a "high water mark" model:

- **Version 4.0 and Above**:

    - Storage is truly elastic—expands and contracts based on data volume.

    - Improved cost optimization.

- **Version 3.6**:

    - Allocated storage only increases.

    - To reclaim unused space, users must perform a logical dump and restore using tools like mongodump and mongorestore.

> **Tip**: To minimize I/O costs during dump and restore operations, consider batch processing and avoid temporary, large-scale ETL workloads that spike storage usage.

Data Replication

Data replication is fundamental to Amazon DocumentDB's high availability and fault tolerance model. Instead of relying on a traditional master-slave replication architecture, Amazon DocumentDB separates compute and storage, allowing for more efficient and robust replication mechanisms.

Six-Way Replication Model

Amazon DocumentDB stores six copies of your data across **three Availability Zones**:

- **2 copies per AZ**

- **3 AZs per Region (minimum)**

This setup ensures that data is both highly available and durable, capable of surviving AZ-level failures.

Replication Characteristics

- **Asynchronous Replication**: Writes made by the primary instance are persisted to the cluster volume and then replicated across AZs.

- **Eventually Consistent Reads**: Replica instances can read from the cluster volume shortly after the primary writes the data. Under normal circumstances, the replica lag is under **100 milliseconds**.

- **No Write Load on Replicas**: Unlike traditional MongoDB deployments, replicas in Amazon DocumentDB do not participate in write propagation. This frees up system resources for read operations and allows for linear read scaling.

Roles of Instances

- **Primary Instance**:

  - The sole writer in the cluster.

  - Handles all modifications to the cluster volume.

- **Replica Instances**:

  - Support read operations only.

  - Scale horizontally (up to 15 replicas per cluster).

  - Can be placed in different AZs for fault tolerance.

Endpoint Design

Amazon DocumentDB provides flexible connection options to leverage its replication model:

1. **Cluster Endpoint**:

    ○ Routes traffic to the current primary.

    ○ Automatically updates on failover.

2. **Reader Endpoint**:

    ○ Load balances across all available replicas.

    ○ Ideal for read-heavy workloads.

3. **Instance Endpoint**:

    ○ Connects to a specific instance (used for specialized tasks like analytics).

> **Best Practice**: Connect using the cluster endpoint in **replica set mode** to take advantage of automatic failover and read scaling. Use the readPreference parameter (e.g., secondaryPreferred) to route reads to replicas.

Crash Recovery

Amazon DocumentDB is engineered for rapid recovery from failures—both expected and unexpected—without compromising data durability or service availability.

Survivable Cache Warming

To reduce the performance impact during recovery, Amazon DocumentDB separates the **database process** from the **page cache process**. This separation allows the page cache to:

- Survive restarts and failures.

- Serve hot data immediately upon instance recovery.

- Reduce the time needed to "warm" the system after a reboot.

Crash Recovery Features

- **Asynchronous, Multi-threaded Recovery**: Upon a failure, DocumentDB doesn't rely on traditional *write-ahead logging (WAL)* or *redo logs* for crash recovery. Instead, the system uses a parallel, multithreaded process to bring the database back online rapidly.

- **Instant Availability**: The database becomes available for reads and writes almost immediately after restart, improving SLA compliance and minimizing downtime.

Storage Auto-Repair

Amazon DocumentDB continuously monitors the cluster volume for signs of corruption or failure. If an error is detected:

- A repair is initiated using healthy data from the remaining replicas.

- Repairs happen transparently and without user intervention.

- The system avoids data loss and the need for user-initiated point-in-time recovery.

Resource Governance and Throttling

Under memory pressure or system resource constraints, Amazon DocumentDB intelligently throttles operations to prioritize essential services like:

- Health checks

- Core system operations

- Cache management

This throttling is tracked using **Amazon CloudWatch** metrics, such as:

- LowMemThrottleQueueDepth

- LowMemNumOperationsThrottled

- LowMemNumOperationsTimedOut

Recommendation: If you observe sustained throttling, consider **scaling up your instance**

class to provide more memory for your workload.

Summary

Amazon DocumentDB's storage and replication model combines the best of modern cloud-native design principles with the robust reliability expected from enterprise-grade database systems. By decoupling compute from storage and replicating data across multiple AZs, it delivers:

- **High availability** through multi-AZ redundancy

- **Cost-efficient scalability** with elastic SSD-backed storage

- **Resilience** via automated crash recovery and cache warming

- **Seamless failover** with endpoint abstraction and replica awareness

Whether you're building a mission-critical application or managing a dynamic, high-throughput document store, Amazon DocumentDB provides the underlying storage and replication framework to support your operational goals with minimal maintenance overhead.

Chapter 7: Endpoints and Connection Models

Cluster, Reader, and Instance Endpoints
Replica Set Mode

Overview

In Amazon DocumentDB (with MongoDB compatibility), managing connections efficiently is essential for application performance, resilience, and scalability. Amazon DocumentDB offers multiple connection endpoints tailored for different use cases. Understanding the functionality and best use of each endpoint type—**Cluster**, **Reader**, and **Instance endpoints**—as well as the **Replica Set Mode**—enables developers to design fault-tolerant and high-performance applications.

This chapter explains how each endpoint functions, how to connect using them, the best practices associated with each, and how Replica Set Mode enhances read consistency and failover handling. The goal is to help architects, developers, and DBAs make informed decisions about their connection strategies in production and development environments.

Cluster Endpoints

A **cluster endpoint** serves as the main gateway to a DocumentDB cluster's **primary instance**. This is the endpoint your applications should use for **read and write**

operations, as it always resolves to the current writer node of the cluster.

Characteristics

- Always connects to the **primary (writer)** instance.

- Supports **read and write** operations.

- Automatically redirects to the new primary in the event of a failover.

- Consistent DNS name even after topology changes.

Syntax Example

sample-cluster.cluster-123456789012.us-east-1.docdb.amazonaws.com:27017

MongoDB URI Format

mongodb://username:password@sample-cluster.cluster-123456789012.us-east-1.docdb.amazonaws.com:27017

Use Cases

- Applications performing **create, update, and delete (CRUD)** operations.

- Systems requiring **strong read-after-write consistency**.

- Clients that expect **automatic failover** handling without endpoint changes.

Benefits

- **High availability**: Seamlessly redirects to a new primary after failover.

- **Simplicity**: One consistent connection string.

- **Durability**: Writes are committed only when stored across a majority of nodes.

Reader Endpoints

A **reader endpoint** is designed to distribute **read-only workloads** across all **replica instances** in the cluster. It acts as a load balancer for read operations but **does not distribute individual read queries**—rather, it balances incoming connections among replicas.

Characteristics

- Connects to **replica instances** (and the primary if it's the only node).

- Supports **read-only** operations.

- Automatically includes new replicas as they become available.

- Not suitable for writes; attempting a write will result in an error.

Syntax Example

sample-cluster.cluster-ro-123456789012.us-east-1.docdb.amazonaws.com:27017

MongoDB URI Format

mongodb://username:password@sample-cluster.cluster-ro-123456789012.us-east-1.docdb.amazonaws.com:27017

Considerations

- **Only balances connections**, not individual queries.

- Can connect to the primary if it's the only instance.

- Best used in **read-heavy workloads** like reporting, analytics, or dashboards.

Benefits

- **Improved read scalability**.

- **Automatic integration of replicas**.

- Reduces load on the primary instance.

Instance Endpoints

An **instance endpoint** connects directly to a specific Amazon DocumentDB instance—whether it is the primary or a replica. This gives you **fine-grained control** over which instance your application communicates with.

Characteristics

- Each instance has its own unique endpoint.

- Can be used for **read** (any instance) or **write** (only the primary).

- Does not support automatic redirection in failover.

- Best for **targeted workloads** like one-off analytics or dedicated job processing.

Syntax Example

sample-instance.123456789012.us-east-1.docdb.amazonaws.com:27017

MongoDB URI Format

mongodb://username:password@sample-
instance.123456789012.us-east-
1.docdb.amazonaws.com:27017

Use Cases

- Connecting to a large replica for **heavy analytics**
  jobs.

- Manually distributing reads across specific replicas.

- Specialized workloads that should avoid impacting
  shared resources.

Limitations

- **Not failover-aware**: If the instance goes down or is
  demoted, the connection fails.

- **Not recommended** for general application use or
  production workloads.

Tip

Never assume a specific instance is always
the primary. Use **cluster endpoints** with
replica set mode for production-grade
applications.

Replica Set Mode

Replica Set Mode is a **connection configuration** that allows clients to treat an Amazon DocumentDB cluster as a **MongoDB replica set**. This enables **advanced read/write behaviors**, including configurable **read preferences**, **write concerns**, and **failover awareness**.

How to Enable

Use the replicaSet=rs0 parameter in your connection string:

mongodb://username:password@sample-cluster.cluster-123456789012.us-east-1.docdb.amazonaws.com:27017/?replicaSet=rs0

Benefits

- Enables support for:

  - **Read preferences** (primary, secondary, secondaryPreferred, etc.)

  - **Write concerns** (implicitly treated as w:3, j:true)

  - **Strong consistency guarantees**

- Enables **automatic recognition of added/removed instances**.

- Provides **client-side failover capabilities**.

Important Notes

- Amazon DocumentDB supports a **single replica set**, always named rs0.

- Connecting in replica set mode is **strongly recommended** for:

  - Production applications

  - High availability requirements

  - Applications with **read scaling** strategies

Read Preferences

Amazon DocumentDB supports several **read preference options** when connected in **replica set mode**:

1. **primary**

   - All reads go to the primary.

   - Provides **strong read-after-write** consistency.

   - Fails if the primary is unavailable.

2. **primaryPreferred**

   - Reads go to the primary if available; otherwise, to replicas.

- Useful during failover scenarios.

3. **secondary**

   - All reads go to replicas.

   - Not suitable if strong consistency is required.

4. **secondaryPreferred**

   - Reads go to replicas if available; otherwise, to the primary.

   - Useful for balancing load while maintaining availability.

5. **nearest**

   - Routes reads to the instance with **lowest network latency**.

   - Can be useful in geographically distributed systems.

Example: Setting Read Preference in Code (Python)

```
from pymongo import MongoClient, ReadPreference

client = MongoClient(
    'mongodb://username:password@sample-
cluster.cluster-123456789012.us-east-
1.docdb.amazonaws.com:27017/?replicaSet=rs0',
```

```
read_preference=ReadPreference.SECONDARY_PREFE
RRED
)

db = client['mydb']
collection = db['mycollection']
print(collection.find_one())
```

Failover Behavior and Best Practices

Amazon DocumentDB uses **automated failover mechanisms** to maintain availability. Applications connected via the **cluster endpoint** in **replica set mode** are automatically redirected during failover.

Best Practices

- Always use **cluster endpoint + replicaSet=rs0** in production.

- Use **read preferences** to balance workloads and increase throughput.

- Avoid using **instance endpoints** unless absolutely necessary.

- Configure **timeouts and retries** in clients to handle failover events gracefully.

- Monitor **replica lag metrics** using Amazon CloudWatch for latency-sensitive apps.

Connection Error Handling

Applications should be designed to handle:

- **Primary failover** (temporary disconnections)

- **DNS resolution delays**

- **Replica lag effects** for eventual consistency

- **Throttle or queue under memory pressure**

Tip

> Use driver-level retry mechanisms and configure **connectTimeoutMS** and **socketTimeoutMS** appropriately.

Summary

Choosing the right endpoint and connection model is fundamental to achieving performance, scalability, and availability in Amazon DocumentDB. The **cluster endpoint** is ideal for general workloads, the **reader endpoint** suits read-heavy operations, and **instance endpoints** allow targeted access. **Replica Set Mode** unlocks advanced connection capabilities, including failover awareness and read preference tuning.

By following best practices and understanding each endpoint's behavior, developers and architects can confidently design robust applications on Amazon DocumentDB that scale and perform under demanding conditions.

Chapter 8: Read and Write Consistency Models

Read Preferences

Read preferences in Amazon DocumentDB define how your application routes read operations across the instances in your cluster. They offer a mechanism to balance between read consistency, latency, and availability.

Amazon DocumentDB is built on a unique architecture that separates compute and storage. This allows it to deliver high durability and availability without needing a traditional multi-node replication set for write durability. However, read scaling is achieved by distributing read operations to multiple replica instances. Read preferences are the primary tool for controlling how reads are routed in such environments.

Supported Read Preference Modes

Amazon DocumentDB supports several read preference options when reading data from the cluster endpoint in replica set mode (?replicaSet=rs0). These preferences impact which instance—primary or replica—handles a read request:

1. **primary**

   - All reads are routed to the primary instance.

   - Offers **strong read-after-write consistency**.

- If the primary is unavailable, the read operation fails.

- Use this mode when strict consistency is paramount (e.g., financial or critical transactional systems).

Example:

db.collection.find().readPref("primary")

2.
3. **primaryPreferred**

- Reads are sent to the primary if available, otherwise routed to a replica.

- Offers strong consistency under normal conditions but can degrade to eventual consistency during failovers.

4. **secondary**

- Routes all reads to a replica instance.

- Provides **eventual consistency**.

- Improves read throughput but not suitable for operations that require the most recent data.

5. **secondaryPreferred**

- Reads prefer replicas, but if none are available, they will go to the primary.

- Useful for applications that prioritize availability and scalability but still need some fallback mechanism.

6. **nearest**

- Not currently supported in Amazon DocumentDB.

Note: Amazon DocumentDB does not support setting tag sets as part of the read preference configuration, unlike native MongoDB deployments.

Choosing the Right Read Preference

Use Case	Recommended Read Preference
Strong read-after-write consistency	primary
Read scaling with fallback	primaryPreferred
Load distribution with relaxed consistency	secondary / secondaryPreferred

Best Practices for Read Preferences

- Always use the **cluster endpoint** in **replica set mode** to benefit from intelligent routing and failover handling.

- For latency-sensitive workloads, benchmark different read preferences to find optimal performance.

- Use **secondaryPreferred** in read-heavy systems where availability and throughput outweigh immediate consistency.

- Monitor **replica lag** using CloudWatch metrics like ReplicaLagMaximum to ensure consistency levels remain acceptable.

Write Durability

Write durability refers to how Amazon DocumentDB ensures that write operations are persistent and not lost, even in the event of failures.

Amazon DocumentDB's durability model is fundamentally different from traditional MongoDB replica sets. Instead of relying on multiple replicas for write acknowledgment, DocumentDB uses a **cloud-native distributed storage layer** that replicates data across three Availability Zones, storing six copies of every piece of data.

Durability Characteristics

- **Writes are acknowledged only after they are safely persisted** to a majority of nodes in the distributed storage system.

- The system ensures durability without requiring w:majority or j:true write concerns, as found in MongoDB.

- **Write concerns are ignored** in Amazon DocumentDB. Any values such as w=1, w=majority, or j=true will not change behavior.

  Amazon DocumentDB is equivalent to using {w:3, j:true} in MongoDB terms, but it is enforced by default and not configurable.

Storage Layer Durability

- Data is written to a **cluster volume**—a virtual, SSD-backed storage system with six-way replication.

- The storage system is **self-healing** and can detect and repair corrupted or missing data segments automatically.

- Snapshots and backups are also durable and consistent, built on this same storage layer.

Implications of Write Durability

- **Single-instance clusters are as durable as multi-instance clusters**, since durability is enforced at the storage layer, not via instance replication.

- **No rollback of acknowledged writes** is possible.

- **No support for non-durable writes** (unlike MongoDB's w:0 or j:false).

Best Practices for Write Durability

- Avoid unnecessary retry logic or concern for wtimeout, as it's not applicable in DocumentDB.

- Focus on optimizing your schema and indexing rather than tuning write concern parameters.

- Use **CloudWatch I/O metrics** to monitor write performance and identify bottlenecks.

Isolation Levels

Isolation levels determine how operations within and across transactions are allowed to interact. They play a critical role in ensuring data correctness in concurrent environments.

Amazon DocumentDB provides an isolation level equivalent to **read committed**, with no support for user-configurable isolation levels at the time of writing.

Transaction Isolation Model

- Amazon DocumentDB uses **multi-version concurrency control (MVCC)** internally.

- All reads within a transaction see a **consistent snapshot** of the data as it existed at the start of the transaction.

- **Writes within a transaction are only visible** after the transaction is committed.

- DocumentDB does **not allow dirty reads**.

Comparison with Traditional Isolation Levels

Isolation Level	Description	Supported in DocumentDB
Read Uncommitted	Allows dirty reads	✗ Not supported
Read Committed	No dirty reads; sees only committed data	✓ Default isolation
Repeatable Read	Same query returns the same results within a transaction	⚠ Partially supported
Serializable	Full isolation like transactions were serial	✗ Not supported

Note: While Amazon DocumentDB supports multi-statement and multi-document transactions, its concurrency control is limited to read-committed semantics.

Implications for Developers

- Use **multi-statement transactions** when you need multiple operations to succeed or fail as a unit.

- Avoid relying on **write skew** or other anomalies that might be prevented by serializable isolation.

- Consider **optimistic concurrency** strategies like versioning in application logic if stronger isolation is required.

Best Practices for Isolation

- Minimize the duration of transactions to reduce contention.

- Avoid long-running read transactions when using secondary read preferences.

- Monitor transaction metrics via CloudWatch (TransactionsStarted, TransactionsAborted, TransactionsCommitted) for tuning.

Summary and Recommendations

Amazon DocumentDB simplifies many aspects of consistency and durability by enforcing high standards at the system level:

- **All writes are highly durable**, regardless of the number of instances in your cluster.

- **Read preferences** provide flexibility in balancing consistency and latency.

- **Read-after-write consistency** is available through the primary instance.

- **Eventually consistent reads** can be offloaded to replicas using secondary preferences.

- **Read committed isolation** ensures reliable and clean reads without dirty data access.

By understanding and leveraging these consistency models effectively, you can build scalable, resilient, and high-performance applications on top of Amazon DocumentDB.

Part III – Working with Documents

Chapter 9: Document Database Essentials

What is a Document Database?

A **document database** is a type of NoSQL database designed to store, retrieve, and manage semi-structured data as documents. Unlike relational databases that store data in rows and columns, document databases use a flexible, JSON-like format (commonly BSON—Binary JSON) to represent data structures.

This model aligns naturally with how modern applications structure their data. Each document is a self-contained unit of data that can include nested structures, arrays, and varying fields—making document databases particularly effective for evolving application requirements.

Key Characteristics

- **Schema Flexibility**: Documents within a collection do not require a uniform schema. Fields can be added or removed without needing to alter a centralized schema definition.

- **Nested Data Support**: Supports complex, hierarchical data natively, using embedded documents and arrays.

- **Rich Query Capabilities**: Despite being schema-less, document databases like Amazon DocumentDB support powerful query capabilities, including filtering, aggregation, indexing, and full-text search.

- **Horizontal Scalability**: Many document databases support sharding for distributed deployments.

- **Atomicity at the Document Level**: Operations on a single document are typically atomic.

Comparison with Other Data Models

Feature	Relational DB	Document DB
Data format	Tables, Rows	JSON-like Documents
Schema	Strict	Flexible
Relationships	Joins, Foreign Keys	Embedded or Referenced
Transactions	Multi-row/ACID	Single-document atomicity, multi-document supported in some engines
Use case fit	OLTP, structured data	Content management, user profiles, catalogs

Amazon DocumentDB (with MongoDB compatibility) is purpose-built to support document-based workloads at scale in the cloud.

Use Cases and Patterns

Document databases are used in a variety of industries and application domains. Amazon DocumentDB is well-suited for workloads that require flexibility, performance, and scalability with document-style data.

Let's explore key patterns and use cases:

Content Management Systems (CMS)

Description

CMS platforms need to manage various types of content: articles, blog posts, pages, user comments, and metadata. These often have different structures that evolve over time.

Why DocumentDB Works

- Documents naturally map to content types with unique attributes.

- Embedding comments or tags within a document avoids complex joins.

- Schema flexibility supports evolving metadata needs.

Example

```
{
  "title": "Modern App Architecture",
  "author": "Jane Doe",
  "tags": ["cloud", "NoSQL", "architecture"],
  "comments": [
    {"user": "john", "comment": "Great read!", "timestamp":
"2025-02-15T12:00:00Z"}
  ],
  "published": true
}
```

Product Catalogs and E-Commerce

Description

In e-commerce, each product may have different attributes. For example, a laptop has specifications like RAM and CPU, while clothing items have size and fabric information.

Benefits

- Schema-less design allows each product to include different attributes.

- Fast read/write performance supports high traffic loads.

- Embedded reviews, inventory data, or promotions can be included in product documents.

Design Tip

Use **embedded documents** for tightly bound data (e.g., reviews) and **referenced documents** for shared entities (e.g., suppliers).

User Profiles and Personalization

Description

Storing user profiles, preferences, and activity logs is another natural fit. Profiles may evolve with new settings or preferences.

Why DocumentDB Fits

- Easy to store nested preferences and activity logs.

- Profiles can be quickly queried and updated as a single unit.

- Read scaling allows personalization at large scale.

Example Document

```
{
  "userId": "u123",
  "name": "Alice",
  "preferences": {
    "theme": "dark",
    "notifications": {
      "email": true,
      "sms": false
    }
  },
  "recentActivity": ["viewed_product_101",
"added_to_cart_202"]
}
```

IoT and Time Series Workloads

Description

IoT systems collect continuous streams of data from sensors or devices. Each record might vary based on the device type.

Benefits of Amazon DocumentDB

- Stores device logs as individual documents.

- TTL (Time-To-Live) support helps with automatic cleanup of outdated entries.

- Supports time-series-like workloads with scalable storage and indexing.

TTL Deletes in Amazon DocumentDB

Amazon DocumentDB provides TTL (Time To Live) indexing to automatically delete documents after a specified period. This is essential for managing large volumes of transient IoT data.

```
{
  "deviceId": "sensor-999",
  "temperature": 22.4,
  "timestamp": ISODate("2025-03-01T10:00:00Z"),
  "expireAt": ISODate("2025-04-01T10:00:00Z")
}
```

🔍 **Pro Tip**: TTL deletes are evaluated once per minute and can be monitored using CloudWatch metrics. For efficient TTL behavior, ensure you index the expiration field.

Event Logging and Audit Trails

Description

Applications often log events, user actions, and system metrics for auditing, debugging, or analytics.

Advantages with DocumentDB

- Flexible event schemas

- Easy ingestion from microservices or serverless pipelines

- Indexed fields like eventType, userId, or timestamp support efficient queries

Sample Audit Event

```
{
  "eventId": "evt-2025-03-1001",
  "eventType": "LOGIN_ATTEMPT",
  "userId": "alice",
  "timestamp": "2025-03-27T08:00:00Z",
  "status": "SUCCESS"
}
```

Amazon DocumentDB integrates well with change streams and can pipe audit logs to Amazon OpenSearch or S3 for real-time search and archival.

Mobile and Web Applications

Description

Front-end applications often need data structures that match their component models—like users, posts, notifications—without complex joins or transformations.

Why DocumentDB is Ideal

- Documents map 1:1 to frontend component state.

- Fast queries and write performance for real-time interactivity.

- Offline-first capabilities with local data caching and sync.

Usage Pattern

- Use DocumentDB as the primary backend for storing application state and content.

- Combine with GraphQL APIs or REST endpoints for flexibility.

Gaming and Leaderboards

Description

Gaming applications generate large volumes of user-centric data—scores, achievements, inventories, and sessions.

DocumentDB Use Cases

- Track player profiles, game sessions, inventory, and events in documents.

- Embed achievements or scores in user documents.

- Efficiently query leaderboards with proper indexing strategies.

Performance Consideration

For real-time leaderboards, consider using materialized views or periodically exported summaries, especially if you're dealing with millions of updates per minute.

Modeling Patterns in Document Databases

When modeling data in a document database, selecting the right structure is essential for performance and maintainability.

Embedding vs Referencing

Approach	Description	When to Use
Embedding	Include nested data in the same document	One-to-few relationships, tightly bound data
Referencing	Store related data in separate documents with references (IDs)	One-to-many or many-to-many relationships, shared or large sub-documents

Schema Design Tips

- **Design for your read patterns**: Optimize for common queries, not strict normalization.

- **Use compound indexes**: Combine fields in indexes to support composite queries.

- **Avoid unbounded arrays**: Large arrays can degrade performance.

- **Watch index selectivity**: High selectivity improves performance; monitor using explain plans.

Best Practices for DocumentDB Use Cases

- Use **Amazon CloudWatch** to monitor performance, memory, and I/O metrics.

- Implement **read replicas** to scale read workloads.

- Leverage **change streams** for real-time data pipelines (e.g., syncing to OpenSearch).

- Use **index analysis tools** to detect unused or missing indexes.

- Employ **IAM roles and encryption** to secure document data at rest and in transit.

Document Modeling in Amazon DocumentDB

Amazon DocumentDB offers MongoDB compatibility, so you can use familiar tools and APIs for modeling, indexing, and querying documents.

Supported Features

- **BSON format** with support for nested structures

- **Rich query language** with $match, $project, $lookup, etc.

- **Aggregation pipelines** for data transformation and analytics

- **Transactions and multi-document operations**

Example Aggregation

```
db.orders.aggregate([
  { $match: { status: "shipped" }},
  { $group: { _id: "$customerId", total: { $sum: "$amount" }}}
])
```

Limitations and Considerations

- Amazon DocumentDB does not support all MongoDB features (e.g., capped collections, some geospatial queries).

- Writes must be directed to the primary instance; replicas are read-only.

- Query performance depends on proper indexing and document size.

Summary

Document databases are a powerful tool for modern application development, offering schema flexibility, scalability, and natural data modeling for JSON-based structures. Amazon DocumentDB extends this power with a fully managed, MongoDB-compatible platform optimized for AWS workloads.

When designing applications with Amazon DocumentDB, it's essential to model data around application access patterns, use indexing effectively, and take advantage of features like TTL, replicas, and change streams to build resilient and performant systems.

Whether you're building a personalized user platform, IoT backend, or CMS, Amazon DocumentDB provides the right foundation to manage your document data at scale.

Chapter 10: Understanding and Modeling Documents

Schema Design Principles

Embedded vs Referenced Documents

In Amazon DocumentDB (with MongoDB compatibility), documents form the core data structure, and how you model those documents significantly impacts performance, flexibility, and scalability. This chapter explores key schema design principles, the use of embedded versus referenced documents, and best practices for modeling documents in a way that maximizes the benefits of Amazon DocumentDB's capabilities.

Understanding Document Structure

A *document* in Amazon DocumentDB is a flexible, JSON-like structure that stores data in key-value pairs. This flexible schema allows developers to store documents with varying structures in the same collection.

Key characteristics of documents in DocumentDB:

- Documents are stored in BSON (Binary JSON) format, allowing for richer data types such as dates and binary data.

- Documents can contain nested documents and arrays.

- Each document has a unique _id field that acts as a primary key.

Example Document

```
{
  "_id": "user123",
  "name": "Jane Doe",
  "email": "jane.doe@example.com",
  "address": {
    "street": "123 Maple Ave",
    "city": "Springfield",
    "state": "IL",
    "zip": "62704"
  },
  "orders": [
    {"order_id": "1001", "amount": 45.00, "status":
"shipped"},
    {"order_id": "1002", "amount": 30.00, "status":
"processing"}
  ]
}
```

This structure illustrates embedded documents (address) and arrays of embedded documents (orders), showcasing DocumentDB's flexibility.

Schema Design Principles

When designing schemas for Amazon DocumentDB, the goal is to balance performance, maintainability, and data access patterns. Consider these principles:

1. Design Around Your Queries

Design schemas based on how your application queries the data, not just how it logically relates. Denormalization (i.e., embedding data) can improve read performance by reducing the number of queries.

2. Data Access Patterns

Optimize for frequent access patterns. If your application often retrieves a user and their recent orders together, embedding orders inside user documents makes sense.

3. Avoid Over-Embedding

Embedding too much data can lead to large documents. Amazon DocumentDB supports documents up to 16 MB, but large documents can cause issues with memory and I/O performance.

4. Favor Atomic Operations

DocumentDB supports atomic operations on single documents. Keeping related data in the same document enables atomic reads and writes.

5. Balance Read and Write Performance

Embedded documents optimize reads, while references offer better write and update performance. Consider trade-offs based on use case.

Embedded Documents

Embedded documents are nested structures stored within a parent document. They are ideal when related data is mostly accessed together.

Benefits

- Fewer queries and joins.

- Atomic operations on related data.

- Efficient for read-heavy workloads with related entities.

Example Use Case

A blog application where each post includes comments:

```
{
  "_id": "post1",
  "title": "Document Modeling",
  "content": "Understanding embedding...",
  "comments": [
    {
      "user": "userA",
      "comment": "Great post!",
      "timestamp": "2025-03-01T10:00:00Z"
    },
    {
      "user": "userB",
      "comment": "Very informative.",
      "timestamp": "2025-03-02T11:30:00Z"
    }
```

```
    ]
}
```

All the comments are embedded inside the post document, optimizing for read operations where the post and its comments are fetched together.

Limitations

- Document size growth is a concern.

- Complex updates may require rewriting the entire embedded array.

- Not suitable for data frequently accessed independently or in large quantities.

Referenced Documents

Referenced documents store relationships between documents using document identifiers. This approach separates data into multiple collections and uses references (_id values) to associate related data.

Benefits

- Better normalization and data integrity.

- More efficient for write-heavy or independently accessed entities.

- Avoids large document sizes.

Example Use Case

A user and their orders stored in separate collections:

User Document

```
{
  "_id": "user123",
  "name": "Jane Doe",
  "email": "jane.doe@example.com"
}
```

Order Document

```
{
  "_id": "order1001",
  "user_id": "user123",
  "amount": 45.00,
  "status": "shipped"
}
```

This approach allows efficient queries for all orders regardless of the user and supports updates to orders independently of the user.

Limitations

- Requires multiple queries or application-side joins.

- Not atomic across multiple documents.

- Potentially slower reads for combined data.

Comparing Embedded and Referenced Models

Criteria	Embedded	Referenced
Performance	Better for reads	Better for writes
Atomicity	Supported on entire document	Only per document
Data Duplication	None	Possible
Ease of Access	Easier for nested data	Requires additional queries
Flexibility	Less flexible for independent access	More flexible
Size Limitations	Risk of exceeding 16 MB	No size issues per se

Choosing Between Embedded and Referenced

Use **embedded documents** when:

- You frequently retrieve the parent and child data together.

- Child data is not frequently updated independently.

- Child documents are limited in size and number.

Use **referenced documents** when:

- Child documents are large or numerous.

- Child entities are accessed independently.

- You need to enforce data normalization or avoid data duplication.

Modeling Relationships

Amazon DocumentDB supports both one-to-one, one-to-many, and many-to-many relationships. The design decision depends on the relationship cardinality and query patterns.

One-to-One

- Embed if the data is conceptually part of the parent.

- Reference if stored separately or updated frequently.

One-to-Many

- Embed if the number of child documents is small and grows slowly.

- Reference if many children or frequent changes are expected.

Many-to-Many

- Use referencing on both sides, often with a join collection to manage the relationship.

Best Practices

1. **Analyze Query Patterns**

   ○ Understand your application's read and write frequency.

2. **Limit Document Size**

   ○ Avoid designs that could exceed the 16 MB document limit.

3. **Use Indexes Wisely**

   ○ Consider compound and multi-key indexes for arrays and embedded fields.

4. **Consider Read Preference**

   ○ For large datasets, referencing works better with secondaryPreferred read settings for better scalability.

5. **Plan for Growth**

   ○ Design schemas that scale as your data grows.

Tips for Schema Evolution

Amazon DocumentDB's flexible schema allows changes over time, but planning helps reduce future friction.

Tip: Use version fields (schema_version) in documents to manage transitions gracefully.

Tip: Avoid schema drift by enforcing JSON schema validation when needed.

Tools and Utilities

- Use the bsondump, mongoexport, and mongoimport tools to analyze and transform documents.

- Amazon DocumentDB supports **JSON Schema Validation**, allowing you to define and enforce structure.

Example JSON Schema Validation Rule

```
{
  "$jsonSchema": {
    "bsonType": "object",
    "required": ["name", "email"],
    "properties": {
      "name": {
        "bsonType": "string"
      },
```

```
    "email": {
      "bsonType": "string",
      "pattern": "^.+@.+$"
    }
   }
  }
}
```

Summary

Modeling documents effectively in Amazon DocumentDB is
foundational for achieving performance, flexibility, and
maintainability. By understanding your application's query
and update patterns, you can make informed decisions
about embedding or referencing documents. Embedding is
ideal for tightly coupled data accessed together, while
referencing shines when data needs to remain flexible,
scalable, and independently addressable.

Use schema design principles strategically to create a
robust document model that scales with your application
and evolves with changing business requirements.

Chapter 11: CRUD and Querying

Insert, Update, Query Basics

CRUD—Create, Read, Update, and Delete—operations are fundamental to working with any database, and Amazon DocumentDB (with MongoDB compatibility) is no exception. This chapter focuses on how to perform basic CRUD operations in Amazon DocumentDB and how to query data effectively using built-in operators and projections. Whether you're building microservices, managing product catalogs, or logging application events, mastering these operations is essential.

Creating Documents (Insert Operations)

Documents in Amazon DocumentDB are BSON-encoded JSON objects stored in collections within databases. To create documents, the insertOne() and insertMany() methods are used.

Example: Insert a single document

```
db.users.insertOne({
  name: "Alice",
  email: "alice@example.com",
  age: 29,
  preferences: {
    language: "en",
    timezone: "UTC+1"
  }
});
```

Example: Insert multiple documents

```
db.users.insertMany([
  { name: "Bob", age: 35 },
  { name: "Carol", age: 42, location: "Paris" }
]);
```

Tips:

- Every document must have a unique _id field. If not provided, Amazon DocumentDB automatically generates an ObjectId.

- Use insertMany() to optimize bulk inserts for performance.

Reading Documents (Query Operations)

The find() and findOne() methods are used to retrieve documents from a collection.

Example: Find all users over age 30

```
db.users.find({ age: { $gt: 30 } });
```

Example: Find one user by name

```
db.users.findOne({ name: "Alice" });
```

Common use cases:

- Filtering based on field values ($eq, $gt, $in)

- Sorting results (sort())

- Limiting or skipping results (limit(), skip())

Example: Find users and sort by age descending

```
db.users.find().sort({ age: -1 });
```

Updating Documents

To modify existing documents, you can use updateOne(), updateMany(), and replaceOne().

Example: Update Alice's age

```
db.users.updateOne(
  { name: "Alice" },
  { $set: { age: 30 } }
);
```

Example: Update all users with age > 40

```
db.users.updateMany(
  { age: { $gt: 40 } },
  { $set: { status: "senior" } }
);
```

Example: Replace an entire document

```
db.users.replaceOne(
  { name: "Bob" },
  { name: "Bob", age: 36, location: "Berlin" }
);
```

Update operators (explained below) allow for fine-grained updates without overwriting entire documents.

Deleting Documents

To remove documents from a collection, use deleteOne() or deleteMany().

Example: Delete one user

```
db.users.deleteOne({ name: "Carol" });
```

Example: Delete users under age 25

```
db.users.deleteMany({ age: { $lt: 25 } });
```

Operators and Projections

Amazon DocumentDB supports a wide array of operators that enhance the power of queries and updates. Operators are used within query filters and updates, while projections are used to specify which fields to include or exclude in the results.

Query Operators

Operators allow you to perform sophisticated queries based on field values.

Comparison Operators

- $eq: Equal to

- $ne: Not equal to

- $gt: Greater than

- $gte: Greater than or equal to

- $lt: Less than

- $lte: Less than or equal to

Example: Find users aged 30 or older

```
db.users.find({ age: { $gte: 30 } });
```

Logical Operators

- $and: Join query clauses with AND logic

- $or: Join query clauses with OR logic

- $not: Negate a clause

- $nor: Negate multiple clauses

Example: Users in Paris or older than 40

```
db.users.find({
  $or: [{ location: "Paris" }, { age: { $gt: 40 } }]
});
```

Element Operators

- $exists: Checks if a field exists

- $type: Matches based on BSON type

Example: Find users with a "preferences" field

```
db.users.find({ preferences: { $exists: true } });
```

Array Operators

- $in: Matches if value is in array

- $nin: Matches if value is not in array

- $all: Matches arrays containing all specified elements

- $size: Matches arrays by size

Example: Users who prefer English or French

```
db.users.find({ "preferences.language": { $in: ["en", "fr"] } });
```

Evaluation Operators

- $regex: Match text using regular expressions

- $expr: Use aggregation expressions in query

- $mod: Perform modulo operation in match

Update Operators

Update operators modify field values during an update operation.

Field Update Operators

- $set: Assigns a value to a field

- $unset: Removes a field

- $inc: Increments a field

- $rename: Renames a field

Example: Increment age by 1

```
db.users.updateOne(
  { name: "Alice" },
  { $inc: { age: 1 } }
);
```

Array Update Operators

- $push: Append value to array

- $pull: Remove matching value from array

- $addToSet: Add value if it doesn't already exist

- $pop: Remove first or last element from array

Example: Add a new tag

```
db.articles.updateOne(
  { title: "AWS Tips" },
  { $addToSet: { tags: "documentdb" } }
);
```

Projection

Projections allow you to control the fields returned in a query result.

Inclusion

Use 1 to include specific fields:

```
db.users.find(
  { age: { $gt: 30 } },
  { name: 1, age: 1 }
);
```

Exclusion

Use 0 to exclude fields:

```
db.users.find(
  {},
  { _id: 0, preferences: 0 }
);
```

Notes:

- _id is always included unless explicitly excluded.

- You cannot mix inclusion and exclusion (except with _id).

Nested Documents and Arrays

Amazon DocumentDB supports dot notation for accessing and querying nested fields.

Example: Find users in timezone UTC+1

```
db.users.find({ "preferences.timezone": "UTC+1" });
```

Example: Update nested field

```
db.users.updateOne(
  { name: "Alice" },
  { $set: { "preferences.language": "de" } }
);
```

Best Practices for CRUD and Querying

- **Use indexes** on frequently queried fields to improve performance.

- **Avoid unbounded** find() operations on large collections.

- **Project only necessary fields** to reduce response payload.

- **Use** $set **over** replaceOne() to avoid unintentional data loss.

- **Design with schema flexibility**, but maintain consistency where possible.

Summary

This chapter covered the core of working with data in Amazon DocumentDB:

- **Insert documents** with insertOne() or insertMany()

- **Query using powerful operators** for filtering and matching

- **Update documents** with precision using operators like $set, $inc, and $push

- **Delete documents** with deleteOne() or deleteMany()

- **Leverage projections** to return only needed fields

Understanding these operations is crucial to building responsive, efficient applications on Amazon DocumentDB. In the next chapter, we'll look at **working with indexes**, and how to optimize query performance through proper indexing strategies.

Chapter 12: Indexing and Aggregation

Index Types, Aggregation Pipelines, and Query Optimization

Amazon DocumentDB supports advanced indexing and aggregation capabilities that enable powerful, performant querying of semi-structured data. Understanding the mechanics of indexes and aggregation pipelines—and how they interact with the query planner—is essential for building scalable applications.

This chapter explores the different **index types**, how to use **aggregation pipelines** effectively, and best practices for **query optimization** in Amazon DocumentDB.

Index Types

Indexes in Amazon DocumentDB are critical for improving query performance. Without indexes, queries must perform a **collection scan**, which can be slow for large datasets. Indexes allow the query engine to locate documents faster based on indexed fields.

Types of Indexes

Amazon DocumentDB supports the following index types:

1. **Single-Field Indexes**

   o   Created on a single field in a document.

- Improves query performance for equality and range queries.

Syntax:

```
db.collection.createIndex({ field: 1 })
```

-

2. **Compound Indexes**

- Indexes that include **two or more fields**.

- The order of fields is significant.

- Ideal for supporting queries that filter or sort on multiple fields.

Syntax:

```
db.collection.createIndex({ field1: 1, field2: -1 })
```

-

3. **Multikey Indexes**

- Automatically created when indexing **array fields**.

- Amazon DocumentDB creates an index entry for each element of the array.

- Useful for queries that search array contents.

4. **Hashed Indexes**

   - Used for sharding in MongoDB but **not supported** in Amazon DocumentDB as of the latest version.

5. **Text Indexes**

   - Allow full-text search on string content.

   - Must be created on string fields.

   - Amazon DocumentDB supports **basic text indexing** with the $text operator.

Syntax:

```
db.collection.createIndex({ content: "text" })
```

   ○
6. **Partial Indexes**

   - Index only a subset of documents based on a filter expression.

   - Useful to optimize space and performance when only a portion of documents are queried frequently.

Syntax:

```
db.collection.createIndex({ field: 1 }, {
partialFilterExpression: { status: { $eq: "active" } } })
```

    o

7. **TTL (Time to Live) Indexes**

    o   Automatically remove documents after a specified time.

    o   Good for expiring session data or temporary records.

Syntax:

```
db.collection.createIndex({ createdAt: 1 }, {
expireAfterSeconds: 3600 })
```

    o

Index Management

- **Identify missing indexes** using profiling or explain() results.

- **Drop unused indexes** to improve write performance and reduce storage.

- Use the reIndex command to rebuild indexes if performance degrades.

Aggregation Pipelines

Aggregation in Amazon DocumentDB uses a **pipeline-based framework**, similar to MongoDB, to transform and analyze data within collections.

An aggregation pipeline is a sequence of **stages**, where each stage performs a specific operation and passes its output to the next stage.

Basic Aggregation Example

```
db.orders.aggregate([
  { $match: { status: "delivered" } },
  { $group: { _id: "$customerId", total: { $sum: "$amount" } }
},
  { $sort: { total: -1 } }
])
```

This pipeline:

1. Filters documents where status is "delivered"

2. Groups by customerId, summing the amount

3. Sorts results by total amount in descending order

Common Aggregation Stages

Stage	Purpose
$match	Filters documents (similar to find())

131

$group	Aggregates values (e.g., $sum, $avg)
$sort	Orders documents
$project	Includes/excludes fields, creates new ones
$limit	Limits number of documents passed
$skip	Skips a number of documents
$unwind	Deconstructs array fields
$lookup	Performs a left outer join (limited support)

Expressions and Operators

Amazon DocumentDB supports many **aggregation expressions**, including:

- **Arithmetic**: $add, $subtract, $multiply, $divide

- **Conditional**: $cond, $ifNull

- **String**: $concat, $substr, $toLower

- **Date**: $year, $month, $dayOfWeek

- **Set**: $setEquals, $setIntersection

Limitations

While aggregation in DocumentDB is robust, it is **not fully identical** to MongoDB:

- Some stages and expressions are partially supported or unavailable.

- $lookup has **functional differences** and limited join capabilities.

- The **maximum aggregation memory** per stage is limited—avoid operations that load large working sets.

Query Optimization

Efficient querying is a key part of performance tuning in Amazon DocumentDB. The system uses a query planner and optimizer to select the best strategy based on indexes and query structure.

Query Planner Basics

You can inspect how a query will be executed using explain():

```
db.collection.find({ status: "active" }).explain()
```

This provides details such as:

- Whether an index was used

- Number of documents scanned vs. returned

- Query stages and execution time

Query Plan Stages

Common plan stages include:

- **COLLSCAN**: Collection scan (no index used)

- **IXSCAN**: Index scan

- **FETCH**: Fetch document after index match

- **SORT**: In-memory sort (try to avoid if possible)

Best Practices for Optimization

1. **Use Indexes Strategically**

   - Create indexes that match your most common query patterns.

   - Use **compound indexes** for multi-field filters and sorts.

2. **Avoid In-Memory Sorting**

   - Always try to match your query's sort order to an existing index.

3. **Use Covered Queries**

   - If all fields in your query are in the index, DocumentDB can return results without

134

accessing the actual documents (faster).

Example:

```
db.products.find({ category: "tools" }, { category: 1, price: 1,
_id: 0 })
```

-
4. **Filter Early in Aggregation**

   - Use $match as early as possible in the pipeline to reduce data processed in later stages.

5. **Monitor with Performance Tools**

   - Use **Amazon CloudWatch** metrics like:

     - DatabaseConnections

     - QueryThroughput

     - FreeableMemory

   - Enable **profiler** for long-running queries.

6. **Avoid Negation and Non-Sargable Queries**

   - Queries using $ne, $nin, or regular expressions without prefixes are hard to optimize.

7. **Paginate Efficiently**

   ○ Avoid deep offsets with $skip and use range queries on indexed fields instead.

Example: Optimized Query with Index

```
// Index:
db.orders.createIndex({ customerId: 1, orderDate: -1 })

// Query:
db.orders.find({ customerId: 123 }).sort({ orderDate: -1 }).limit(10)
```

This example uses an **index that covers both the filter and the sort**, resulting in highly efficient execution.

Indexing and Aggregation Together

Indexing can dramatically improve the performance of aggregation pipelines. For example:

- Using an index on the $match stage's fields reduces the number of documents passed to later stages.

- Sorting in the pipeline without an index incurs in-memory sorting, which is slow and resource-intensive.

Real-World Example

```
// Index
db.logs.createIndex({ userId: 1, timestamp: -1 })

// Aggregation
db.logs.aggregate([
  { $match: { userId: 123 } },
  { $sort: { timestamp: -1 } },
  { $limit: 5 }
])
```

Because of the index, this aggregation is highly performant.

Tools and Monitoring

Amazon DocumentDB provides several tools to identify and optimize performance issues:

- **CloudWatch Metrics**

    - Monitor key indicators like ReadLatency, WriteThroughput, and ReplicationLag.

- **Profiler**

    - Enable slow query logging and review long-running operations.

- **Performance Insights**

- Provides a dashboard with real-time query analysis.

- **CloudTrail**

  - Tracks API calls and configuration changes.

Summary

Effective indexing and aggregation design is essential for building fast and scalable applications on Amazon DocumentDB.

Key takeaways:

- Use **single-field, compound, and multikey indexes** to match your access patterns.

- Apply **partial and TTL indexes** where applicable for performance and data lifecycle management.

- **Aggregation pipelines** allow complex transformations and summaries, but must be tuned carefully.

- Use the **query planner (**explain**)** to guide optimization efforts.

- Monitor performance continuously using **CloudWatch, Profiler, and Performance Insights**.

Mastering these capabilities will allow you to deliver applications that scale efficiently and meet user expectations for speed and responsiveness.

Part IV – Getting Started and Deployment

Chapter 13: Getting Started

Prerequisites

Before diving into the creation and use of Amazon DocumentDB clusters, it's essential to understand the foundational requirements that ensure a smooth and secure setup. Amazon DocumentDB is a fully managed, MongoDB-compatible database service designed to run in a Virtual Private Cloud (VPC). Therefore, preparing your environment beforehand is critical for connectivity, performance, and security.

Here are the primary prerequisites to get started:

1. AWS Account

To use Amazon DocumentDB, you must have an **active AWS account**. If you do not already have one, visit aws.amazon.com and sign up. You may also be eligible for the free trial described in Chapter 3.

2. AWS Identity and Access Management (IAM)

IAM allows you to securely control access to AWS resources, including Amazon DocumentDB. You'll need:

- An **IAM user or role** with permissions to create and manage DocumentDB resources.

- IAM policies attached to your user or group that allow the necessary actions such as docdb:CreateDBCluster, docdb:CreateDBInstance, ec2:DescribeSecurityGroups, and cloudwatch:* for monitoring.

Tip: For initial setup, using the AmazonDocumentDBFullAccess managed policy is recommended.

3. Virtual Private Cloud (VPC)

Amazon DocumentDB clusters are deployed within an **Amazon VPC**, which provides network isolation and security. You'll need:

- An existing VPC or permissions to create one.

- At least **two subnets in different Availability Zones**, preferably three for high availability.

- A properly configured **security group** to allow inbound and outbound connections (typically on port 27017 for MongoDB protocol).

Note: DocumentDB does not support public IPs. All connectivity must be routed through a VPC endpoint or VPN/Direct Connect.

4. Amazon EC2 (for connectivity)

To connect to your Amazon DocumentDB cluster, you typically need an **Amazon EC2 instance** in the same VPC:

- This instance acts as a client to connect to the cluster using MongoDB tools and drivers.

- You'll also need an EC2 **key pair** to SSH into the instance.

Optional but recommended:

- Enable **Session Manager** or **bastion host access** for secure administrative access.

- Configure IAM roles for the EC2 instance if you plan to access AWS resources from it.

5. MongoDB Tools and Drivers

Amazon DocumentDB is compatible with MongoDB APIs, so you'll use MongoDB-compatible tools for client connections:

- **Mongo Shell** (mongo)

- **MongoDB Compass** or GUI tools like **Studio 3T** and **DataGrip**

- Supported programming language **MongoDB drivers** (Python, Java, Node.js, Go, etc.)

6. SSL/TLS Certificates

Amazon DocumentDB **requires TLS** connections by default. You must:

- Download the **rds-combined-ca-bundle.pem** certificate from AWS.

- Provide the certificate when connecting via command-line tools or programmatically.

7. Region and Instance Class Selection

Choose a **region** close to your application for minimal latency. Not all **instance classes** are available in every region, so verify your desired configuration is supported using the AWS documentation.

8. Client Machine Setup (Local or EC2)

To connect locally (outside AWS), ensure:

- You have **VPC peering** or **VPN/Direct Connect** in place.

- Your firewall and routing settings permit access to the DocumentDB cluster endpoint.

To connect via EC2:

- Install required client libraries and SSL certificates.

- Open port 27017 in the EC2 security group for DocumentDB communication.

Step-by-Step Cluster Setup

Amazon DocumentDB provides multiple ways to create clusters, including through the AWS Management Console, AWS CLI, and CloudFormation templates. This section outlines the **console-based setup**, which is the most intuitive for beginners.

Step 1: Sign in to the AWS Management Console

1. Open https://console.aws.amazon.com and sign in with an IAM user or role that has necessary permissions.

2. Navigate to **Amazon DocumentDB** under the "Database" category.

Step 2: Create a Cluster

1. Choose **Create** under the "Clusters" section.

2. Select your desired **MongoDB compatibility version** (e.g., MongoDB 5.0).

3. Provide a **Cluster Identifier** (e.g., dev-cluster-01).

4. Under **Credential Settings**, provide:

   ○ A **master username** (e.g., docdbadmin)

   ○ A **master password** (must meet AWS security requirements)

Step 3: Configure Instances

1. Select the **Instance Class** — this determines the compute and memory size (e.g., db.r5.large).

2. Choose the **number of instances**:

   ○ At least **1 primary**

   ○ Up to **15 read replicas** for scaling reads

3. For high availability, deploy replicas in different **Availability Zones**.

Step 4: Configure Connectivity

1. Select a **VPC**.

2. Choose at least **2 subnets** in different Availability Zones.

3. Select a **VPC security group**:

   ○ Make sure the security group allows inbound connections on port 27017 from your client (e.g., EC2).

Tip: Avoid using the default security group in production; define custom rules for access control.

Step 5: Enable Encryption (Optional)

- Check the box to **enable encryption at rest** using AWS Key Management Service (KMS).

- Select a KMS key or use the default AWS-managed key.

Step 6: Configure Backup and Maintenance

1. Set the **backup retention period** (1–35 days).

2. Define your **preferred backup window** (optional).

3. Choose a **maintenance window** to control when updates and patches occur.

Step 7: Enable or Disable Monitoring Features

- Enable **Enhanced Monitoring** and **Performance Insights** for better observability.

- Configure **CloudWatch logs** for diagnostics and auditing.

Step 8: Review and Create

- Review all your configurations on the final screen.

- Click **Create Cluster** to launch the setup.

It typically takes **5–10 minutes** for the cluster and its instances to become available.

Post-Creation: Connect to the Cluster

Once your cluster is active:

1. Navigate to the **cluster details page**.

2. Locate the **Cluster Endpoint** and **Reader Endpoint**.

Download the **SSL certificate** if not already done:

```
curl https://s3.amazonaws.com/rds-downloads/rds-combined-ca-bundle.pem -o rds-combined-ca-bundle.pem
```

3.

Connect via Mongo Shell (from EC2):

```
mongo "mongodb://<username>:<password>@<cluster-endpoint>:27017/?ssl=true&replicaSet=rs0&readPreference=secondaryPreferred&retryWrites=false" --sslCAFile rds-combined-ca-bundle.pem
```

Replace <username>, <password>, and <cluster-endpoint> with your values.

Connect using Python (PyMongo):

```
from pymongo import MongoClient

client = MongoClient(
    "mongodb://<username>:<password>@<cluster-endpoint>:27017/?ssl=true&replicaSet=rs0&readPreference=secondaryPreferred",
```

```
    tls=True,
    tlsCAFile='rds-combined-ca-bundle.pem'
)

db = client.testdb
print(db.list_collection_names())
```

Best Practices for Initial Setup

- **Use replica set mode** for all connections to leverage failover and read scaling.

- **Use a bastion host** or **VPN** for secure access if connecting from on-prem or outside AWS.

- **Implement monitoring early** to track usage, performance, and errors.

- **Automate setup** using CloudFormation or Terraform for consistency across environments.

- **Establish IAM roles and secrets management** for production authentication practices.

What's Next?

After setting up your Amazon DocumentDB cluster:

- Begin **inserting and querying data** using MongoDB tools or programming language drivers.

- Explore **monitoring and diagnostics** in CloudWatch.

- Implement **backup strategies** and **IAM access policies**.

- Plan for **indexing**, **query tuning**, and **cost optimization**.

Chapter 14: Quick Start with CloudFormation

Templates, IAM Setup, EC2 Key Pairs

Introduction

Amazon DocumentDB provides a powerful managed NoSQL database solution compatible with MongoDB. While you can set up Amazon DocumentDB manually using the AWS Management Console or CLI, leveraging AWS **CloudFormation** significantly accelerates and automates the deployment process. This chapter presents a **Quick Start guide** using CloudFormation to provision a DocumentDB cluster, with detailed coverage on required templates, IAM permissions, and Amazon EC2 key pairs.

Using CloudFormation not only standardizes your deployments across environments but also ensures repeatability, scalability, and security by managing infrastructure as code (IaC).

Benefits of Using CloudFormation for DocumentDB

Deploying DocumentDB with CloudFormation offers several key advantages:

- **Infrastructure as Code (IaC)**: Automate and version-control your database infrastructure.

- **Rapid provisioning**: Launch fully configured DocumentDB clusters in minutes.

- **Consistent environments**: Avoid configuration drift between staging, development, and production.

- **Integrated security**: Define IAM roles, VPC settings, and security groups within the same template.

Prerequisites

Before you launch your CloudFormation stack, ensure the following:

- An active AWS account with sufficient permissions

- A configured EC2 key pair in your AWS Region

- IAM roles and policies allowing CloudFormation and DocumentDB provisioning

- Familiarity with JSON or YAML for editing templates (if needed)

- Amazon VPC with public and private subnets, or be prepared to create one

Templates

AWS provides a **CloudFormation template** for quickly provisioning a DocumentDB cluster along with required networking and security components. You can use the AWS-provided sample or author your own.

Sample Template Components

A typical quick-start template includes:

- **Amazon VPC**: Networking setup with public and private subnets

- **Security Groups**: Allowing access to DocumentDB and EC2 for testing

- **Amazon DocumentDB Cluster**: Primary and optionally replica instances

- **Amazon EC2 Instance**: For connecting to the DocumentDB cluster (bastion host)

- **IAM Roles and Policies**: For CloudFormation and EC2 permissions

- **CloudFormation Parameters**: Such as instance class, DB username, and password

Template Format

Templates can be written in **YAML** or **JSON**. Here's a small snippet of a YAML template defining a basic DocumentDB cluster resource:

```
Resources:
  MyDocumentDBCluster:
    Type: AWS::DocDB::DBCluster
```

```
Properties:
  MasterUsername: !Ref DBUsername
  MasterUserPassword: !Ref DBPassword
  DBClusterIdentifier: my-docdb-cluster
  VpcSecurityGroupIds:
    - !Ref DocumentDBSecurityGroup
  DBSubnetGroupName: !Ref
DocumentDBSubnetGroup
```

Launching the Stack

To launch your DocumentDB CloudFormation stack:

1. Open the AWS Management Console.

2. Navigate to **CloudFormation** > **Create Stack**.

3. Upload your YAML or JSON template.

4. Fill in parameter values such as:

   ○ Database username and password

   ○ Instance class

   ○ Number of replicas

5. Review and confirm the IAM capabilities acknowledgment.

6. Click **Create Stack**.

You can monitor the progress of the stack creation in the console under the "Events" tab.

Output Section

A well-structured template provides **outputs**, such as:

- DocumentDB cluster endpoint

- EC2 bastion host public IP

- IAM role ARN

Example:

```
Outputs:
  ClusterEndpoint:
    Description: "Amazon DocumentDB Cluster Endpoint"
    Value: !GetAtt MyDocumentDBCluster.Endpoint
```

IAM Setup

CloudFormation requires specific IAM permissions to create and manage AWS resources. Without the correct roles or policies, stack creation will fail.

Required IAM Permissions

The IAM user or role launching the stack must have:

- **CloudFormation permissions**: cloudformation:*

- **DocumentDB permissions**:

    - docdb:CreateDBCluster

    - docdb:CreateDBInstance

    - docdb:CreateDBSubnetGroup

- **EC2 permissions**:

    - ec2:CreateSecurityGroup

    - ec2:AuthorizeSecurityGroupIngress

    - ec2:CreateKeyPair

- **IAM permissions** (if roles are being created):

    - iam:PassRole

You can use an IAM policy similar to the following:

```
{
 "Version": "2012-10-17",
 "Statement": [
  {
   "Effect": "Allow",
   "Action": [
    "docdb:*",
    "cloudformation:*",
    "ec2:*",
    "iam:PassRole"
   ],
```

```
  "Resource": "*"
  }
 ]
}
```

Note: In production, it's best to scope down permissions to the minimum required.

Using IAM Roles with CloudFormation

For secure automation:

- Assign a role to the CloudFormation stack with elevated permissions.

- Use **IAM Instance Profiles** for any EC2 bastion hosts if access to Secrets Manager or other AWS services is required.

IAM Best Practices

- Always enable **least privilege**: grant only the permissions needed.

- Rotate IAM credentials regularly.

- Use **CloudFormation service roles** for separation of duties.

EC2 Key Pairs

An **EC2 key pair** is required if your CloudFormation stack provisions an EC2 instance to connect to DocumentDB. This instance often serves as a bastion host in a public subnet.

Creating a Key Pair

1. Navigate to **EC2 Console** > **Key Pairs**.

2. Click **Create Key Pair**.

3. Choose a name (e.g., my-docdb-key).

4. Select file format: .pem (Linux/macOS) or .ppk (Windows with PuTTY).

5. Download and save it securely—you won't be able to access it again.

Referencing Key Pair in CloudFormation

Your template must reference the key pair name in the EC2 resource:

```
Resources:
  BastionHost:
    Type: AWS::EC2::Instance
    Properties:
      InstanceType: t3.micro
      KeyName: !Ref EC2KeyPairName
      ImageId: ami-0abcdef1234567890
```

Include a parameter to allow dynamic key selection:

```
Parameters:
  EC2KeyPairName:
    Description: "Name of an existing EC2 KeyPair to
enable SSH access"
    Type: "AWS::EC2::KeyPair::KeyName"
```

Connecting to the Bastion Host

Once your EC2 instance is running:

```
ssh -i my-docdb-key.pem ec2-user@<EC2-Public-IP>
```

From this host, you can use MongoDB tools or drivers to connect to your DocumentDB cluster.

Validating the Deployment

Once the stack is complete, validate your deployment by:

1. Reviewing the **Outputs** in CloudFormation.

2. Logging into the EC2 instance using your key pair.

3. Connecting to the DocumentDB cluster using mongo shell or application code.

4. Verifying that security groups and VPC configurations allow access.

5. Exploring CloudWatch for basic monitoring.

Cleanup and Deletion

To avoid unnecessary charges:

- Delete the CloudFormation stack after testing (Delete Stack from the console).

- Ensure snapshots, logs, and unused security groups are removed.

- Manually delete any retained resources not managed by CloudFormation.

Tips & Best Practices

- **Use parameterized templates** for flexibility across environments.

- **Tag your resources** via CloudFormation for cost tracking.

- **Use nested stacks** for large deployments (e.g., network stack + DocumentDB stack).

- **Secure credentials** using AWS Secrets Manager instead of hardcoding in templates.

- **Limit public access** by using private subnets and bastion hosts.

- **Integrate CloudFormation into CI/CD pipelines** for continuous deployment.

Summary

This quick-start guide demonstrates how to leverage AWS CloudFormation to deploy Amazon DocumentDB in a reliable, repeatable, and secure manner. By combining templates, proper IAM configuration, and EC2 key management, teams can streamline their database provisioning and align with modern DevOps practices. Whether for development, testing, or production environments, CloudFormation offers a scalable path to infrastructure automation.

Part V – Compatibility and Extensions

Chapter 15: Elastic Clusters

Elastic Clusters in Amazon DocumentDB represent a major leap in database scalability and performance for modern applications. Designed to handle millions of reads and writes per second and scale to petabytes of storage, Elastic Clusters are the ideal solution for use cases that exceed the limits of traditional instance-based clusters. This chapter explores the core components of Elastic Clusters, real-world use cases, the principles of sharding and scaling, and best practices for managing connections in high-throughput environments.

Use Cases

Elastic Clusters are tailored for applications that require **massive scale, high throughput, and low latency**, without compromising on availability or durability. Below are some key use cases where Elastic Clusters shine.

High-Volume Operational Workloads

Elastic Clusters are ideal for operational applications where high transaction volume and concurrent connections are common. Examples include:

- **E-commerce platforms**: Managing product catalogs, orders, inventory, and user data across regions.

- **Online gaming platforms**: Handling real-time player stats, matchmaking, leaderboards, and in-game transactions.

- **Financial services**: Powering high-frequency trading platforms, transaction logs, and real-time fraud detection systems.

Time-Series and Event Data

Applications that generate and consume time-series data benefit significantly from the performance and partitioning Elastic Clusters provide.

- **IoT telemetry ingestion**: Devices sending millions of updates per second across a wide geographic footprint.

- **Log aggregation and analytics**: Systems collecting and analyzing logs from various services for observability and security.

Generative AI and ML Workloads

Modern AI applications often require a scalable backend for storing vector embeddings, metadata, and inference results. Elastic Clusters support:

- **Vector search use cases**: Retrieval-augmented generation (RAG), recommendation engines, similarity search.

- **No-code ML platforms**: Integrating with SageMaker Canvas for building ML models without writing code.

Multi-Tenant SaaS Architectures

Elastic Clusters support **sharded collections**, which naturally align with tenant-based architectures:

- Isolating workloads by tenant using shard keys.

- Optimizing resource allocation and query efficiency.

Archival and Historical Data Access

When petabytes of structured or semi-structured documents need to be stored and occasionally queried, Elastic Clusters offer scalable storage with indexing support and cost-efficiency.

Sharding and Scaling

Elastic Clusters achieve scalability through **sharding**, a data partitioning technique that distributes data across multiple nodes or "shards." Sharding in Amazon DocumentDB Elastic Clusters is **transparent and managed**, allowing you to scale with minimal operational overhead.

What is Sharding?

Sharding is the process of splitting a collection into subsets based on a **shard key**, and distributing those subsets across multiple compute and storage nodes (shards). Each shard handles a subset of the overall data and its associated queries.

Sharded Collections

When you shard a collection in an Elastic Cluster, Amazon DocumentDB:

1. Splits the data based on the configured **shard key**.

2. Distributes the partitions (chunks) across shards.

3. Automatically balances and redistributes data as your dataset grows or usage patterns change.

Example: Sharding a collection

```
db.adminCommand({
  shardCollection: "mydb.mycollection",
  key: { userId: 1 }
});
```

Choosing a Shard Key

Choosing the right shard key is critical for:

- Ensuring **even distribution** of data across shards.

- Preventing **hotspots** where one shard receives disproportionate load.

- Supporting **query performance** by targeting a minimal number of shards.

Best practices for choosing a shard key:

- Use high-cardinality fields (e.g., userId, deviceId)

- Avoid monotonically increasing values (e.g., timestamps)

- Consider compound keys for multidimensional queries

Scaling Elastic Clusters

Elastic Clusters can **scale horizontally** by adding or removing shards, based on your throughput and storage needs.

Horizontal Scaling Features

- **Compute scaling**: Scale read/write throughput linearly by adding more shards.

- **Storage scaling**: Expand up to **petabytes** of storage capacity with minimal impact.

- **Online rebalancing**: Automatically redistribute data across shards when topology changes.

Tip: Elastic Clusters vs. Instance-Based Clusters

Feature	Elastic Clusters	Instance-Based Clusters
Maximum Storage	Petabytes	128 TiB
Read/Write Throughput	Millions/sec	Tens of thousands/sec
Scaling Mode	Horizontal (shard-level)	Vertical (instance size change)
Sharded Collections	Required	Not supported
High-Volume Workloads	Optimized	Limited

Connection Best Practices

Effectively managing client connections is crucial in a distributed environment. The Elastic Clusters architecture introduces a few nuances compared to standard DocumentDB clusters.

Use Replica Set Mode

Elastic Clusters expose a **replica set-style endpoint** for connecting. Clients should connect using the replicaSet=rs0 parameter to:

- Enable **read preference** options

- Allow the driver to manage **failovers** and **read routing**

- Maintain **connection resiliency**

Example MongoDB URI

```
mongodb://username:password@my-
cluster.docdb.elastic.aws-
region.amazonaws.com:27017/?replicaSet=rs0
```

Pool Connections Efficiently

To maximize performance:

- Use **connection pooling** at the application level.

- Avoid opening and closing connections for each request.

- Tune pool size based on workload and driver recommendations.

Distribute Workloads Across Shards

Elastic Clusters route queries to shards based on the **shard key** in the query filter. For optimal performance:

- Include the shard key in read/write queries.

- Avoid scatter-gather queries that touch all shards.

- Use **range-based** or **hash-based** partitioning based on access patterns.

Monitor and Adapt

Use **CloudWatch metrics** and **Performance Insights** to:

- Track query latency and error rates.

- Detect skewed workloads across shards.

- Identify long-running operations or high replica lag.

Use TLS and IAM Authentication

As with all DocumentDB connections:

- Always enable **TLS** for secure data in transit.

- Use **IAM authentication** for secure and auditable access control.

Handle Failovers Gracefully

Elastic Clusters handle failovers automatically, but applications must:

- Avoid relying on **fixed IPs or hostnames**.

- Reconnect using the cluster endpoint with retry logic.

- Handle **transient connection errors** gracefully.

Summary

Amazon DocumentDB Elastic Clusters provide a powerful foundation for building highly scalable, performant, and resilient document-based applications. By understanding the **use cases**, mastering **sharding principles**, and applying **connection best practices**, you can fully harness the capabilities of Elastic Clusters for even the most demanding data workloads.

Chapter 16: MongoDB Compatibility

Supported Versions

Amazon DocumentDB (with MongoDB compatibility) is purpose-built to support MongoDB workloads by providing wire protocol compatibility, allowing applications to interact with DocumentDB using MongoDB drivers and tools. As of 2025, Amazon DocumentDB supports the following MongoDB versions:

- **MongoDB 3.6**

- **MongoDB 4.0**

- **MongoDB 5.0**

Each version includes varying levels of feature parity and specific functional differences. Amazon DocumentDB does not run MongoDB software; instead, it implements its own purpose-built architecture to provide compatibility and scalability for document database workloads at cloud scale.

Compatibility Layers

Amazon DocumentDB achieves compatibility by implementing:

- **MongoDB wire protocol**: Enables client-driver communication.

- **Supported MongoDB APIs**: Includes read/write operations, aggregation pipelines, and query syntax.

- **Schema-less data modeling**: Just like MongoDB, data is stored in flexible JSON-like documents (BSON).

Version-Specific Highlights

- **MongoDB 5.0 Compatibility**:

    o Latest major compatibility layer.

    o Includes support for enhanced aggregation features, nested projection, and partial indexing.

    o Introduces support for **$vectorSearch**, a generative AI feature for semantic search use cases.

    o Enhanced performance improvements in replica scaling and query execution.

- **MongoDB 4.0 Compatibility**:

    o Support for multi-document transactions.

    o Better consistency controls with causal consistency.

    o Improved change streams support.

- **MongoDB 3.6 Compatibility**:

- Baseline for initial DocumentDB releases.

- Includes support for JSON schema validation, TTL indexes, and change streams.

- Storage and resource utilization follow the "high water mark" allocation model.

Note: Amazon DocumentDB does not support MongoDB 6.0 or newer as of the current release.

Functional Differences

While Amazon DocumentDB strives for compatibility, it is not a drop-in replacement for every MongoDB feature. There are several **functional differences** in supported features, operations, and behaviors that developers must be aware of during migration or integration.

Notable Differences

1. **Write Concern and Durability**:

   - DocumentDB provides **always-durable** writes (effectively w:3, j:true).

   - Ignores write concern parameters like wtimeout, j, or lower durability settings.

   - You cannot reduce the write durability level.

172

2. **Read Preferences**:

   - Supports primary, primaryPreferred, secondary, secondaryPreferred, and nearest.

   - Does **not support** read preference tag sets.

3. **Transactions**:

   - Supported from MongoDB 4.0 and above in DocumentDB.

   - Transactions are atomic across multiple documents and collections.

   - Transactions can use **callback APIs** or **core APIs** with session support.

4. **Aggregation Pipeline**:

   - Wide support for MongoDB pipeline stages and expressions.

   - Includes operators such as $match, $project, $group, $lookup, and $vectorSearch.

   - Some advanced operators (e.g., $function, $accumulator) are not supported.

5. **Change Streams**:

- Available from MongoDB 3.6 onward.

- Enable real-time tracking of changes to collections.

- Amazon DocumentDB change streams support filtering, resume tokens, and integration with AWS services like **Lambda** and **OpenSearch**.

6. **Authentication & Access Control**:

   - RBAC with built-in and user-defined roles.

   - Integration with AWS IAM for identity-based access.

   - **Does not support** MongoDB's x.509 certificate-based authentication.

7. **Unsupported Features**:

   - Sharding: Instead, Amazon DocumentDB provides **Elastic Clusters** for horizontal scaling.

   - Server-side JavaScript.

   - Certain MongoDB admin commands (e.g., fsync, repairDatabase, etc.).

   - Direct manipulation of the admin database or low-level system collections.

Feature Comparison Table (Summary)

Feature	MongoDB	DocumentDB
Multi-document Transactions	✓	✓
$lookup (Join)	✓	✓ (Partial)
$vectorSearch	✗	✓
Change Streams	✓	✓
Sharding	✓	✗ (Use Elastic Clusters)
Full Text Search	✓	✓ (with differences)
Geospatial Queries	✓	✓
Schema Validation	✓	✓
ACID Transactions	✓	✓ (within limitations)

> **Tip**: Always refer to the Amazon DocumentDB Feature Compatibility Matrix for up-to-date support status.

Migration Strategies

Migrating from a MongoDB deployment to Amazon DocumentDB requires careful planning, especially in light of functional differences and operational models. There are several recommended migration paths, based on your current workload, architecture, and uptime requirements.

1. Offline Migration

Best suited for applications that can tolerate downtime during migration.

- **Step-by-step**:

  - Export data using mongodump.

  - Create an Amazon DocumentDB cluster.

  - Restore data using mongorestore.

  - Recreate indexes and validate schema.

  - Point your application to the new endpoint.

- **Considerations**:

  - Simple and repeatable.

  - Good for development, testing, or non-critical workloads.

  - May incur downtime.

2. Online Migration with AWS DMS

Ideal for minimizing downtime during live migrations.

- **AWS Database Migration Service (DMS)**:

  - Supports full load and change data capture (CDC) from MongoDB to DocumentDB.

- Ensures near real-time replication of changes.

- **Steps**:

  - Enable change streams in the MongoDB source.

  - Configure DMS endpoints and replication tasks.

  - Perform a full load of the source database.

  - Monitor change replication until sync is caught up.

  - Cut over the application endpoint to DocumentDB.

- **Benefits**:

  - Enables zero-downtime cutovers.

  - Robust logging and validation options.

Note: DMS requires MongoDB replica sets and the source to be accessible to the DMS replication instance.

3. Hybrid Migration

Combines aspects of both offline and online strategies.

- **Use Case**:

  - When a full DMS setup isn't feasible.

  - Partial migrations by collection or shard.

- **Approach**:

  - Use mongoexport/mongoimport for static data.

  - Use custom change capture logic or AWS Lambda to replicate ongoing writes.

Index Migration Considerations

- DocumentDB does **not** automatically create the same indexes as the source.

- Use tools or scripts to export and recreate indexes.

- Optimize index strategy to suit DocumentDB's replication and read-scaling architecture.

Testing the Migration

Migration testing is critical before cutover:

- **Unit Tests**: Validate CRUD operations and query outputs.

- **Performance Tests**: Simulate real-world workloads.

- **Failover Tests**: Validate read scaling and resilience.

- **Schema Validation**: Use $jsonSchema or third-party tools to enforce schema correctness.

Cutover Planning

- Use DNS switchover or endpoint reconfiguration to transition applications.

- Monitor CloudWatch metrics (e.g., ReplicaLag, WriteLatency) post-migration.

- Retire old systems gradually after verification.

> **Migration Tip**: For large production workloads, clone a subset of your data and test the migration path before moving the entire dataset. This reduces risk and uncovers any compatibility issues early.

Summary

Amazon DocumentDB provides extensive compatibility with MongoDB, allowing developers to reuse drivers, tools, and application logic with minimal changes. However, understanding the differences and planning for them is essential to a successful transition.

- Supported MongoDB versions: **3.6, 4.0, 5.0**

- Functional differences include read/write concerns, authentication, and aggregation features.

- Migration strategies vary from simple offline dumps to advanced real-time replication with **AWS DMS**.

- Testing, index recreation, and schema validation are vital parts of the migration process.

Chapter 17: Transactions

Multi-Statement and Multi-Collection Isolation, Retryable Writes

Introduction

In modern cloud-native applications, **transactions** provide critical guarantees for **atomicity, consistency, isolation, and durability** (ACID). With support for **multi-statement** and **multi-collection** transactions, **Amazon DocumentDB (with MongoDB compatibility)** empowers developers to build resilient, consistent applications while preserving flexibility and scalability.

This chapter delves into the core transaction features of Amazon DocumentDB, including how to execute multi-statement and multi-collection transactions, how isolation works, and how **retryable writes** enhance fault tolerance. We'll also cover best practices and important limitations to guide your implementation strategy.

Understanding Transactions in Amazon DocumentDB

A **transaction** in Amazon DocumentDB is a sequence of one or more read/write operations that are executed as a **single logical unit of work**. If any part of the transaction fails, the entire set of operations is **rolled back**, leaving the database in a consistent state.

Transactions are supported in both **MongoDB 4.0 and 5.0** compatible versions of DocumentDB.

Key Features

- Support for **multi-document** transactions.

- Ability to perform transactions across **multiple collections** within the same database.

- **Atomicity**: All operations either succeed or none do.

- **Durability**: Once committed, changes persist.

- **Read isolation**: Provides snapshot isolation level.

- **Retryable writes**: Automatically retries idempotent operations in case of transient failures.

Multi-Statement Transactions

A **multi-statement transaction** involves a group of operations—reads and writes—that must succeed or fail together. This is useful in scenarios like order processing, financial transfers, or any multi-step business logic.

Example (Python with PyMongo)

```
from pymongo import MongoClient

client = MongoClient(
    "mongodb://username:password@sample-
cluster.cluster-123456789012.us-east-
1.docdb.amazonaws.com:27017/?replicaSet=rs0"
```

```
)

session = client.start_session()
db = client["ecommerce"]

with session.start_transaction():
    db.orders.insert_one({"order_id": 1001, "total": 250},
session=session)
    db.inventory.update_one({"item_id": "ABC123"}, {"$inc":
{"stock": -1}}, session=session)
```

Characteristics

- Transactions must be explicitly started and committed.

- Any exception during the block will **abort** the transaction.

- Write operations must be directed to the **primary instance**.

Multi-Collection Transactions

Amazon DocumentDB supports transactions across multiple collections **within the same database**. This feature is critical for modeling **normalized relationships** and **data consistency** across related entities.

Use Case Example

Consider a **banking application** transferring funds:

- Debit from accounts collection

- Credit in transactions collection

```
with session.start_transaction():
    db.accounts.update_one({"account_id": "A1"}, {"$inc":
{"balance": -100}}, session=session)
    db.transactions.insert_one({"from": "A1", "to": "A2",
"amount": 100}, session=session)
    db.accounts.update_one({"account_id": "A2"}, {"$inc":
{"balance": 100}}, session=session)
```

Limitations

- Transactions **cannot span multiple databases**.

- Collections involved must exist **prior to the transaction**.

- The number of operations per transaction should remain **within quota limits**.

Isolation in Amazon DocumentDB

Amazon DocumentDB implements **snapshot isolation**, which means:

- Each transaction reads from a **consistent snapshot** of the data as it existed at the start of the transaction.

- Transactions are **serializable** within themselves but may not block or be blocked by other transactions.

Properties

- **Read operations** return data as of the beginning of the transaction.

- **Write operations** are visible only after the transaction commits.

- **No dirty reads**: A transaction never reads uncommitted changes from another transaction.

- **No lost updates**: DocumentDB ensures safe concurrent updates using optimistic concurrency.

Retryable Writes

Retryable writes allow Amazon DocumentDB to **automatically retry** failed write operations without risking duplication. This is especially useful for transient issues like:

- Network timeouts

- Transient instance failovers

- Temporary service interruptions

How It Works

- Each write is tagged with a **unique identifier** by the driver.

- If the operation fails, it can be safely retried using the same identifier.

- The server ensures **idempotency** by detecting and ignoring duplicated operations.

Supported Operations

- insertOne

- updateOne

- replaceOne

- deleteOne

Enabling Retryable Writes

Most modern MongoDB drivers (e.g., PyMongo, Node.js, Java) support retryable writes out of the box when used in **replicaSet mode** with the appropriate parameters.

MongoClient(

```
'mongodb://username:password@cluster.endpoint:27017/?
replicaSet=rs0&retryWrites=true'
)
```

Transaction API Examples

Amazon DocumentDB supports two approaches to
transactions via MongoDB drivers:

1. **Callback API** – Abstracts away manual transaction
   control.

2. **Core API** – Gives full control over session and
   transaction boundaries.

Callback API Example (JavaScript)

```
const session = client.startSession();

try {
  await session.withTransaction(async () => {
    await orders.insertOne({ orderId: 5001 }, { session });
    await inventory.updateOne({ item: "X1" }, { $inc: { qty: -1
} }, { session });
  });
} finally {
  await session.endSession();
}
```

Core API Example (Python)

```
session = client.start_session()

try:
    session.start_transaction()
    db.customers.insert_one({"name": "Alice"},
session=session)
    db.orders.insert_one({"customer": "Alice", "item":
"Book"}, session=session)
    session.commit_transaction()
except Exception:
    session.abort_transaction()
finally:
    session.end_session()
```

Limitations of Transactions

Before implementing transactions in Amazon
DocumentDB, it's important to understand the boundaries:

- Transactions **cannot modify capped collections**
  or system collections.

- **No sharded collection** support for transactions (in
  instance-based clusters).

- Transactions **must complete within 60 seconds**
  or they are aborted.

- Maximum **16 MB** per transaction in total document
  size.

- **High write throughput** within transactions may be throttled under memory pressure.

Monitoring Transactions

Amazon DocumentDB provides several tools to monitor transactions:

- **CloudWatch metrics**:

  - TransactionsInProgress

  - TransactionsCommitted

  - TransactionsAborted

- **Diagnostic logs** show transaction commit or failure events.

- Use the profiler to trace **long-running or blocked transactions**.

Best Practices for Monitoring

- Set **CloudWatch alarms** on abnormal abort or failure rates.

- Use **low TTLs** for short-lived sessions to prevent resource exhaustion.

- Analyze **retry metrics** to detect application resiliency issues.

Best Practices for Transactions

To maximize efficiency and safety with transactions:

- Keep transactions **short-lived** to reduce lock contention.

- Avoid **bulk operations** inside transactions; use batched writes instead.

- Validate all **collections exist** before executing a transaction.

- Always handle **exceptions and retries** gracefully.

- Test transactions under **failover conditions** to ensure robustness.

Tip

Use retryable writes for all critical operations— even outside transactions—to achieve full resilience.

Transaction Use Cases

Transactions in Amazon DocumentDB are applicable to a wide range of real-world applications:

- **E-commerce**: Order and inventory updates.

- **Banking**: Atomic fund transfers and audit logging.

- **Content management systems**: Updating related metadata, tags, and records.

- **SaaS platforms**: Managing user subscriptions and billing simultaneously.

Summary

Amazon DocumentDB's support for transactions delivers the **ACID guarantees** needed for modern application development. With multi-statement and multi-collection capabilities, **snapshot isolation**, and **retryable writes**, developers can ensure data integrity without sacrificing scalability or flexibility.

When used correctly—with awareness of limitations and best practices—transactions become a powerful tool for managing complex data workflows within a distributed, managed database environment like Amazon DocumentDB.

Chapter 18: API, Operators, and Data Types

Supported MongoDB APIs

Amazon DocumentDB is designed to provide MongoDB compatibility, enabling developers to use familiar drivers and tools to interact with the database. However, while it supports many MongoDB APIs, not all are implemented or behave exactly as in MongoDB. This chapter explores the scope of MongoDB API compatibility in Amazon DocumentDB, including supported commands, operators, and data types.

Amazon DocumentDB supports versions 3.6, 4.0, and 5.0 of the MongoDB API, each with incremental feature support. Applications originally built on MongoDB can often migrate to Amazon DocumentDB with little to no code modification, but it's important to understand which APIs and commands are supported or differ functionally.

Overview of Compatibility

Amazon DocumentDB supports:

- Most **CRUD (Create, Read, Update, Delete)** operations.

- A wide range of **aggregation pipeline operators**.

- A robust set of **query and projection operators**.

- Comprehensive support for **indexing**, including compound, partial, and multi-key indexes.

- Basic **session handling**, **retryable writes**, and **transactions**.

- **Geospatial**, **text search**, and **array manipulation** operators.

Notably, DocumentDB does **not support sharding** or features dependent on MongoDB's native distributed cluster capabilities, such as **change streams on sharded collections**, or **MongoDB's** $out **and** $merge operators for writing aggregation results to collections.

Commands and Data Types

Commands are the cornerstone of programmatic interaction with DocumentDB. They include administrative tasks (like creating users), diagnostic operations, and data manipulation commands. DocumentDB supports most of the commonly used MongoDB commands, especially those critical for application development and management.

Administrative Commands

Amazon DocumentDB supports administrative commands such as:

- createUser / dropUser

- createRole / dropRole

- grantRolesToUser

- revokeRolesFromUser

- listDatabases

- listCollections

- dbStats

- collStats

These commands allow database administrators to manage security and understand usage patterns.

Aggregation Commands

DocumentDB includes full support for the aggregate command, allowing developers to use a powerful pipeline-based data processing model.

Common aggregation stages include:

- $match

- $group

- $project

- $sort

- $limit

- $skip

- $unwind

- $lookup (with limitations compared to MongoDB)

  Note: Some aggregation operators like $merge, $out, and $graphLookup are **not supported**.

Authentication and Session Commands

- authenticate

- logout

- startSession

- endSessions

- killAllSessions

Amazon DocumentDB supports **IAM-based authentication**, **username/password authentication**, and **session-based operations**. Integration with **AWS Secrets Manager** is also supported for managing primary user credentials securely.

Diagnostic Commands

- serverStatus

- buildInfo

- ping

- isMaster (aliased as hello in MongoDB 5.0)

These commands are essential for monitoring the health and metadata of the cluster.

Query and Write Commands

Supported commands include:

- find

- insert

- update

- delete

- findAndModify

- count

- distinct

- explain

> **Tip:** You can run explain() on your queries to inspect query plans and identify potential performance improvements.

Role and User Management

All major commands for user and role management are supported:

- createUser, updateUser, dropUser

- createRole, updateRole, dropRole

- grantRolesToUser, revokeRolesFromUser

- usersInfo, rolesInfo

Amazon DocumentDB implements **Role-Based Access Control (RBAC)**, where custom roles can be defined to fit various operational and security requirements.

Supported Operators

Operators are expressions used in queries, updates, and aggregations to transform or filter data.

Query and Projection Operators

Amazon DocumentDB supports a comprehensive list of MongoDB operators used in find() and projection expressions:

Comparison Operators

- $eq, $ne, $gt, $gte, $lt, $lte, $in, $nin

Logical Operators

- $and, $or, $not, $nor

Element Operators

- $exists, $type

Evaluation Operators

- $regex, $mod, $text, $where

Array Operators

- $all, $elemMatch, $size

Projection Operators

- $slice, $elemMatch, $meta, $

Note: DocumentDB has limitations with certain regex indexing and does not support all text index configurations.

Update Operators

Used in update and updateMany operations:

Field Update

- $set, $unset, $rename, $inc, $mul, $min, $max

Array Update

- $push, $pull, $pop, $addToSet, $pullAll

Date and Timestamp

- $currentDate, $timestamp

Amazon DocumentDB supports retryable writes, which enhances write resilience during transient failures.

Aggregation Pipeline Operators

Common Stages

- $match, $group, $project, $sort, $limit, $skip, $unwind, $count, $lookup

Accumulator Expressions

- $sum, $avg, $min, $max, $first, $last, $push, $addToSet

Arithmetic Operators

- $add, $subtract, $multiply, $divide, $mod

Conditional and Type Conversion

- $cond, $ifNull, $switch, $convert, $toString, $toDate

Amazon DocumentDB does not currently support advanced stages like $merge or $out.

Geospatial Operators

Amazon DocumentDB supports basic geospatial capabilities:

- $geoWithin

- $geoIntersects

- $near

- $nearSphere

Along with spatial geometry specifiers like:

- Point, Polygon, MultiPolygon, LineString

Text Search Operators

Amazon DocumentDB supports full-text search via:

- $text: Search a collection using a text index.

- $meta: Return the text score.

Limitations exist around stemming, diacritic handling, and language-specific analysis.

Data Types

Amazon DocumentDB supports a wide range of MongoDB-compatible data types:

BSON Type	Description
Double	Floating-point number
String	UTF-8 encoded string
Object	Embedded document
Array	Ordered list of values
Binary data	Byte array
ObjectId	Unique identifier
Boolean	true or false
Date	UTC datetime
Null	Null value
Int32	32-bit integer
Int64	64-bit integer
Timestamp	Internal timestamp type
Decimal128	High-precision decimal

Amazon DocumentDB does **not support** certain BSON types such as DBRef, JavaScript with scope, **or** Symbol.

Type Conversion

Aggregation pipelines support $convert, $toInt, $toDouble, $toString, etc., for explicit data type transformations.

Special Notes

- ObjectId is automatically generated unless explicitly specified.

- Binary data is supported but should be used cautiously in high-throughput scenarios due to size and encoding considerations.

- Date fields are stored as ISODate values and can be queried using comparison and $date

201

aggregation operators.

Summary and Recommendations

Amazon DocumentDB offers substantial MongoDB API compatibility, particularly for CRUD operations, aggregation, user management, and indexing. While certain advanced MongoDB features are not available (e.g., sharding, $merge, $graphLookup), the platform supports a rich set of commands and data types for building scalable applications.

Recommendations:

- Use the MongoDB 4.0 or 5.0 compatibility mode to access newer aggregation and update operators.

- Leverage explain() and CloudWatch for query diagnostics.

- Consult the official DocumentDB API reference for up-to-date details on command support.

- Avoid unsupported or deprecated features when migrating from MongoDB.

Part VI – Security and Identity

Chapter 19: Security Best Practices

Encryption in Transit and at Rest

Security is foundational to any cloud-based database solution, and Amazon DocumentDB provides robust encryption capabilities to protect your data both **in transit** and **at rest**. These features are designed to help you meet organizational security requirements, industry regulations, and compliance standards.

Amazon DocumentDB uses industry-standard encryption mechanisms integrated with AWS services to simplify key management, enforce secure connections, and provide visibility into encryption events.

Encryption at Rest

Overview

Encryption at rest protects your stored data from unauthorized access when the data is inactive. In Amazon DocumentDB, encryption at rest is handled using **AWS Key Management Service (AWS KMS)**. It encrypts the underlying database storage, automated backups, snapshots, and replica data.

Key Features

- Integrated with **AWS KMS** for centralized key management.

- Uses **AES-256 encryption** algorithm.

- Encryption is **enabled at cluster creation** and cannot be disabled afterward.

- All backups, including **manual snapshots and point-in-time recovery data**, are encrypted using the same key.

- Ensures that **data never appears unencrypted on disk**, including temporary files or internal caches.

Enabling Encryption at Cluster Creation

Encryption at rest can only be enabled during the creation of a new Amazon DocumentDB cluster. You can choose one of the following keys:

- **AWS-managed key (default)** – Managed by AWS and automatically used without additional configuration.

- **Customer managed key (CMK)** – Created and managed in AWS KMS. Offers more control, including:

  - Key rotation

  - Access control via IAM

o Key usage auditing

Considerations

- **Snapshots** of unencrypted clusters cannot be restored to encrypted clusters and vice versa.

- To migrate data to an encrypted cluster, use **logical backup and restore** (e.g., mongodump and mongorestore).

- CMKs provide more visibility and control for compliance-driven workloads.

💡 **Tip**: Rotate your customer-managed keys periodically and audit their usage with AWS CloudTrail for tighter security governance.

Monitoring Encrypted Resources

Use **CloudTrail** and **CloudWatch** to monitor access and activity related to encrypted clusters:

- Track **KMS key usage** in CloudTrail logs.

- Set up **CloudWatch Alarms** to notify on access attempts or key deletion.

- Enable **logging on cluster snapshots** to detect when and how your encrypted data is accessed.

Encryption in Transit

Overview

Encryption in transit ensures that data transferred between your application and Amazon DocumentDB is encrypted using **Transport Layer Security (TLS)**.

TLS prevents eavesdropping, man-in-the-middle attacks, and unauthorized tampering with data during communication.

How It Works

- Amazon DocumentDB requires or optionally supports TLS depending on the configuration.

- TLS uses **X.509 certificates** to verify the server identity.

- Certificates are signed by Amazon's trusted Certificate Authority.

Enforcing TLS

By default, Amazon DocumentDB supports TLS connections. You can configure your client to **require** or **prefer** TLS using connection parameters:

```
mongodb://username:password@cluster-
endpoint:27017/?tls=true
```

For maximum security, configure the connection with the following:

- tls=true

- Specify **CA certificate** (downloadable from AWS)

- Use **replica set mode** (replicaSet=rs0) for high availability and secure routing

Steps to Connect with TLS Enabled

1. **Download the Amazon Root CA certificate**:

   ○ https://truststore.pki.rds.amazonaws.com/global/global-bundle.pem

2. **Update your connection string** with the TLS certificate:

```
mongo --host cluster-endpoint:27017 \
    --tls \
    --tlsCAFile global-bundle.pem \
    --username myUser \
    --password myPassword \
    --authenticationDatabase admin
```

Verifying TLS Connection

- Run db.runCommand({connectionStatus: 1}) in the Mongo shell and inspect the tls field.

- Amazon CloudWatch exposes metrics and logs that can help identify connections over insecure channels (if any are permitted).

Best Practices

- Always require TLS on client-side.

- Regularly rotate client certificates if applicable.

- Automate certificate validation using CI/CD or connection wrapper scripts.

- Enable logging to audit all TLS-based connections.

Secrets Manager

AWS **Secrets Manager** provides a secure and scalable solution for managing and rotating Amazon DocumentDB credentials. Instead of hardcoding sensitive credentials in code or configuration files, developers can retrieve them securely at runtime.

Key Benefits

- Store and retrieve credentials securely via API.

- Automatically **rotate database passwords**.

- Monitor access and usage through CloudTrail.

- Fine-grained **IAM access control**.

- **Integrated with Amazon DocumentDB** for primary user credential management.

Storing DocumentDB Credentials in Secrets Manager

Setup Flow

1. **Create a Secret**:

   - Use the AWS Console or AWS CLI.

   - Choose "Other type of secrets" and enter the DocumentDB credentials.

2. **Configure Access**:

   - Attach IAM policies that permit reading the secret to your EC2, Lambda, or container role.

   - Example IAM policy:

```
{
  "Version": "2012-10-17",
  "Statement": [
    {
      "Effect": "Allow",
      "Action": ["secretsmanager:GetSecretValue"],
```

```
    "Resource": "arn:aws:secretsmanager:us-east-
1:123456789012:secret:docdb-credentials-*"
  }
 ]
}
```

3. **Use AWS SDK or CLI to Retrieve**:

```python
import boto3
import json

client = boto3.client('secretsmanager')
response = client.get_secret_value(SecretId='docdb-
credentials')
credentials = json.loads(response['SecretString'])
```

Automatic Password Rotation

Amazon DocumentDB supports **automatic rotation of the primary user password** using Secrets Manager and AWS Lambda.

Steps to Enable

1. **Store the primary user credentials in Secrets Manager**.

2. Enable rotation and attach a **rotation Lambda function**:

  ◦ AWS provides a blueprint for DocumentDB.

3. The Lambda function:

  ◦ Generates a new password.

  ◦ Updates DocumentDB with the new credentials.

  ◦ Verifies the new credentials.

  ◦ Updates the secret in Secrets Manager.

Benefits

- No downtime or manual steps required.

- Eliminates the risk of hardcoded passwords.

- Supports rotation intervals as low as **one day**.

Monitoring Rotation Activity

Use CloudWatch metrics and logs from Secrets Manager and Lambda to verify:

- Rotation status (Success/Failure)

- Invocation counts

- Credential validation results

Managing Primary User Passwords

You can enforce centralized password management for Amazon DocumentDB clusters by configuring the cluster to **require Secrets Manager integration** for primary user authentication.

Enforcing DocumentDB Password Management

Amazon DocumentDB supports **enforcement of Secrets Manager** as the password authority:

- You can opt in to **enforced password rotation mode** at cluster creation.

- If enabled, manual password changes via CLI or API are blocked.

- Ensures a **single source of truth** for credential management.

Secrets Manager Limitations

While powerful, Secrets Manager integration has several limitations to consider:

- Currently supports **only the primary user** for automated rotation.

- Does not manage **application users or roles**.

- Rotation Lambdas require proper IAM and network access to the cluster (e.g., VPC, subnets).

- Enforced rotation is **only available for new clusters**.

Security Best Practices Summary

To strengthen the security posture of your Amazon DocumentDB environment, adhere to the following best practices:

Encryption

- Always **enable encryption at rest** using AWS KMS.

- Use **customer-managed keys** for compliance-heavy environments.

- Rotate encryption keys regularly and monitor with CloudTrail.

Network and Transport Security

- Require **TLS for all client connections**.

- Use **VPC peering or PrivateLink** to avoid public internet exposure.

- Download and use **Amazon CA certificates** in connection strings.

Credential Management

- Use **AWS Secrets Manager** to store and retrieve credentials.

- Enable **automatic password rotation**.

- Enforce IAM policies to restrict who can access secrets.

Auditing and Monitoring

- Enable **CloudTrail logs** for DocumentDB and Secrets Manager.

- Monitor **TLS usage**, **KMS key activity**, and **password rotation** events.

- Set up **CloudWatch alarms** for security events (e.g., unencrypted connection attempts).

Final Thoughts

Security in Amazon DocumentDB is deeply integrated with AWS services to provide a comprehensive framework for encryption, access control, auditing, and credential management. By combining encryption at rest, TLS encryption in transit, and secure credential rotation through

Secrets Manager, you can build a highly secure and compliant document database environment.

Staying vigilant with continuous monitoring, key rotation, and access control is key to maintaining a secure DocumentDB deployment. Embrace automation where possible to reduce human error and enforce consistent security policies across your infrastructure.

Chapter 20: Identity and Access Management

IAM Integration

Role-Based Access Control (RBAC)

Managing access to Amazon DocumentDB (with MongoDB compatibility) is a critical component of securing your database workloads. This chapter provides an in-depth exploration of Identity and Access Management (IAM) integration with Amazon DocumentDB and how to implement fine-grained access control using Role-Based Access Control (RBAC). Together, these approaches help ensure that only authorized users and services can perform operations in your DocumentDB clusters.

Introduction to Access Control in Amazon DocumentDB

Access control in Amazon DocumentDB consists of two complementary mechanisms:

- **IAM Integration** – Leverages AWS Identity and Access Management to authorize users and roles to access DocumentDB resources at the AWS API level.

- **Role-Based Access Control (RBAC)** – Provides fine-grained control at the database level by managing user roles and associated privileges within a DocumentDB cluster.

While IAM governs who can interact with AWS-level resources (such as creating or modifying a cluster), RBAC defines what actions a user can perform inside the database itself (such as reading collections or creating indexes).

IAM Integration with Amazon DocumentDB

IAM allows you to control access to Amazon DocumentDB clusters using IAM policies, roles, and users. IAM integration is especially useful for securely connecting EC2 instances, Lambda functions, containers, or users without managing database credentials manually.

Benefits of IAM Integration

- Centralized access management across all AWS services.

- Temporary credentials using IAM roles (via STS) for improved security posture.

- Auditability via CloudTrail logging of IAM actions.

- Reduces the need to store and rotate database usernames/passwords.

Authenticating Using IAM

IAM authentication is supported in Amazon DocumentDB using the MongoDB-compatible MONGODB-AWS authentication mechanism.

Key Concepts

- **IAM Role or User**: The identity authenticated by AWS.

- **Temporary Security Credentials**: Generated using the sts:AssumeRole or IAM user permissions.

- **Signature Version 4 (SigV4)**: The signing process that adds AWS credentials to the database connection string.

Steps to Use IAM Authentication

1. **Enable IAM authentication** on your Amazon DocumentDB cluster.

2. **Create a database user** that maps to an IAM role or user ARN.

3. **Assign IAM policies** to allow connecting to DocumentDB.

4. **Connect using a MongoDB driver** that supports the MONGODB-AWS authentication mechanism.

Example Policy for IAM Authentication

```
{
```

```
"Version": "2012-10-17",
"Statement": [
  {
    "Effect": "Allow",
    "Action": "docdb:connect",
    "Resource": "arn:aws:rds-db:us-east-
1:123456789012:dbuser:cluster-
ABC123456/iam_db_user"
  }
 ]
}
```

Drivers that Support IAM Authentication

- Official MongoDB drivers (v3.6+ with MONGODB-
  AWS support).

- AWS SDKs that use SigV4 signing.

- Tools like AWS Secrets Manager for credential
  automation.

Managing IAM Roles and Policies for DocumentDB

IAM Policy Elements

- **Actions**: docdb:* for all actions or specific ones like
  docdb:connect, docdb:CreateDBCluster.

- **Resources**: Use ARNs to specify clusters, users,
  etc.

- **Conditions**: Add context-based restrictions (e.g., IP addresses, tags).

Examples

- **Grant Read-Only Access to a Cluster**

```
{
  "Effect": "Allow",
  "Action": [
    "docdb:Connect"
  ],
  "Resource": "arn:aws:rds-db:us-east-1:123456789012:dbuser:cluster-ABC123456/read_only_user"
}
```

- **Allow Full Cluster Management**

```
{
  "Effect": "Allow",
  "Action": "docdb:*",
  "Resource": "*"
}
```

IAM Authentication Connection String

mongo "mongodb://sample-cluster.cluster-xxxx.us-east-1.docdb.amazonaws.com:27017/?authMechanism=MONGODB-AWS&ssl=true"

Note: IAM authentication only applies to users
created with IAM support enabled inside the
database.

Role-Based Access Control (RBAC)

RBAC provides an internal authorization mechanism that
controls what database users can do once they are
authenticated. It maps users to roles and assigns specific
privileges to those roles.

RBAC Concepts in Amazon DocumentDB

- **User**: A database identity authenticated via
  password or IAM.

- **Role**: A named collection of privileges.

- **Privilege**: A specific operation (e.g., find, insert,
  update) on a namespace (database/collection).

RBAC in DocumentDB is modeled after MongoDB's
access control system but is tailored to Amazon
DocumentDB's security model and supported operations.

Built-In Roles

Amazon DocumentDB provides several predefined roles that simplify common access patterns.

Role	Description
read	Grants read-only access to a specific database.
readWrite	Grants read and write access to a specific database.
dbAdmin	Grants administrative rights to a database (e.g., index creation).
userAdmin	Allows creation and modification of users on a database.
clusterAdmin	Allows administrative actions on the cluster, including all databases.

Example: Assigning a Role

```
db.createUser({
  user: "appUser",
  pwd: "securePassword123",
  roles: [
    { role: "readWrite", db: "ecommerce" }
  ]
});
```

Creating Custom Roles

Amazon DocumentDB allows creation of custom roles for specific access control.

Example: Creating a Custom Role

```
db.createRole({
  role: "orderProcessor",
  privileges: [
    {
      resource: { db: "sales", collection: "orders" },
```

222

```
    actions: [ "find", "update" ]
   }
 ],
 roles: []
});
```

Assigning the Role

```
db.createUser({
  user: "orderUser",
  pwd: "complexPwd!",
  roles: [ { role: "orderProcessor", db: "sales" } ]
});
```

Managing Users in DocumentDB

Amazon DocumentDB requires at least one **primary user** per cluster (usually master or admin), created during cluster provisioning.

Creating Additional Users

```
db.createUser({
  user: "analyst",
  pwd: "analyticsPwd!",
  roles: [ { role: "read", db: "analytics" } ]
});
```

Viewing Users and Roles

```
db.getUsers();
db.getRoles({ showPrivileges: true });
```

Dropping Users or Roles

```
db.dropUser("analyst");
db.dropRole("orderProcessor");
```

IAM + RBAC: Combining Both Approaches

You can use IAM for **authentication** and RBAC for **authorization**, providing a layered security model.

Use Case Example

1. An application runs on EC2 with an attached IAM role.

2. The IAM role is allowed to connect to DocumentDB.

3. Inside DocumentDB, a user mapped to that role exists with limited RBAC permissions (e.g., read-only access to analytics).

Best Practices for IAM and RBAC

- **Principle of Least Privilege**: Grant only necessary permissions.

- **Use IAM Roles for Applications**: Avoid hardcoding credentials.

- **Rotate Passwords and Keys**: Use AWS Secrets Manager or similar tooling.

- **Use Custom Roles for Fine-Grained Control**: Especially in multi-tenant or segmented environments.

- **Monitor Access Logs**: Enable CloudTrail and DocumentDB logging.

Monitoring and Auditing Access

Amazon DocumentDB supports:

- **CloudTrail Logging** – Logs IAM actions (e.g., connect, create cluster).

- **Audit Logs** – Record DML operations like inserts, updates, and deletes.

- **CloudWatch Metrics** – Monitor connections, throttling, auth attempts.

Enable and monitor:

- AuthenticationFailures

- ConnectionCount

- LowMemNumOperationsThrottled (IAM auth-related memory pressure)

Limitations and Considerations

- IAM and RBAC are **not interchangeable**. IAM handles AWS-level access; RBAC handles in-cluster permissions.

- **IAM authentication does not support all MongoDB tools** (check for driver compatibility).

- Password-based users are still required for some tooling (e.g., mongodump).

Summary

Amazon DocumentDB's security model combines AWS IAM for secure authentication with Role-Based Access Control (RBAC) for precise authorization. This layered approach enables strong, manageable, and auditable access controls across infrastructure and data. Whether you're managing applications, analytics users, or admin access, leveraging both IAM and RBAC together provides the flexibility and security needed for enterprise-grade deployments.

Chapter 21: Auditing and Logging

Event Streams

Auditing and logging are crucial components of any secure and compliant data platform. In Amazon DocumentDB (with MongoDB compatibility), auditing helps organizations meet regulatory requirements, monitor access patterns, and troubleshoot suspicious or unauthorized activity. Amazon DocumentDB provides a robust, built-in audit logging system that tracks various database events in real-time.

What Is Auditing in Amazon DocumentDB?

Auditing in Amazon DocumentDB refers to the capture of user-initiated operations and events performed on your database. This includes data definition language (DDL), data manipulation language (DML), authentication events, and access attempts. These events are recorded as logs, which can be stored, queried, or exported for downstream processing and analysis.

Auditing supports tracking actions like:

- Connection attempts and authentication

- User role changes and permission grants

- Creation and deletion of collections or databases

- DML operations such as insert, update, and delete

Benefits of Event-Based Auditing

- **Security & Compliance:** Maintain a detailed record of who accessed your system and what actions were taken.

- **Forensics:** Understand what happened before or during a security event.

- **Operational Monitoring:** Track usage patterns and behavior anomalies.

- **Regulatory Alignment:** Meet requirements such as SOC 2, HIPAA, GDPR, or FedRAMP.

Types of Audited Events

Audit logs in Amazon DocumentDB record the following categories:

- **Authentication Events:** Successful and failed connection attempts.

- **Authorization Events:** User privilege escalations, role assignments.

- **DML Operations:** Insert, update, delete operations.

- **DDL Operations:** Creation or deletion of users, collections, indexes.

- **Administrative Events:** Parameter changes, cluster events.

Enabling Audit Logging

To enable auditing, you must modify the cluster's parameter group:

1. Go to the **Amazon DocumentDB Console**.

2. Choose your cluster and locate its **parameter group**.

3. Modify the audit_logs parameter:

    ○ Set it to enabled to begin logging.

4. Apply changes and restart the cluster if required.

Important: Enabling audit logs may impact performance and storage, so it's recommended to enable it selectively and monitor impact closely.

Accessing Audit Logs

Amazon DocumentDB audit logs are written to Amazon CloudWatch Logs. You can:

- View logs in **CloudWatch Logs Insights**.

- Export logs to **Amazon S3** for archival or integration with SIEM systems.

- Use **AWS CLI or SDK** to download and analyze logs programmatically.

Example AWS CLI to get log stream names:

```
aws logs describe-log-streams \
  --log-group-name "/aws/docdb/cluster/my-cluster/audit"
```

Log Format and Fields

Each audit log entry is a structured JSON document containing:

- timestamp: Time of the event

- user: Database user performing the action

- action: Type of operation (e.g., insert, delete, createCollection)

- database: Affected database

- collection: Affected collection

- success: Boolean indicating outcome

- source: IP or endpoint origin

Example Log Entry:

```
{
  "timestamp": "2025-03-21T14:55:22Z",
  "user": "admin",
  "action": "createCollection",
  "database": "users_db",
  "collection": "user_profiles",
  "success": true,
  "source": "10.0.0.15"
}
```

Best Practices for Audit Logging

- Enable only the categories of events needed to minimize overhead.

- Use **log retention policies** in CloudWatch to control storage costs.

- Integrate logs with **AWS CloudTrail**, **Amazon Athena**, or **OpenSearch** for analytics.

- Regularly review access logs for anomalies.

- Restrict who can read and modify audit logs using **IAM policies**.

Monitoring Access and DML

Monitoring who is accessing your database, from where, and what they're doing is a cornerstone of good operational security. Amazon DocumentDB provides multiple features to help you monitor access and DML (Data Manipulation Language) operations beyond audit logs.

Access Monitoring Overview

To monitor access patterns and activity, Amazon DocumentDB integrates with:

- **Amazon CloudTrail:** Logs API calls to the DocumentDB service.

- **Amazon CloudWatch Metrics:** Provides real-time system health indicators.

- **Performance Insights:** Visual dashboard for long-running queries and wait events.

- **Profiler Logs:** Capture query-level activity in detail.

Using CloudTrail for Access Monitoring

Amazon CloudTrail records API calls made to Amazon DocumentDB, including who made the call, when, and from where. These records are particularly helpful for:

- Tracing configuration changes

- Monitoring administrative access

- Alerting on unusual API usage

Example Events Tracked in CloudTrail:

- CreateDBCluster

- DeleteDBInstance

- ModifyDBParameterGroup

- AuthorizeDBSecurityGroupIngress

You can search and filter CloudTrail logs using the AWS Console or Amazon Athena.

Monitoring DML Operations

DML operations include insert, update, and delete. These operations can be monitored in multiple ways:

1. Audit Logs (recommended)

As discussed, audit logs track every DML event when enabled.

233

2. Profiler

Enabling the Profiler allows you to track operations in more detail:

- Slow queries

- Long-running updates

- Expensive deletes

To enable the profiler:

1. Set profiler parameter to enabled in the cluster's parameter group.

2. Access profiler logs via CloudWatch.

Log Example:

```
{
  "ts": "2025-03-21T15:15:42Z",
  "ns": "orders_db.orders",
  "command": "update",
  "millis": 251,
  "query": { "orderStatus": "pending" },
  "updateObj": { "$set": { "orderStatus": "shipped" } }
}
```

3. Performance Insights

Use this dashboard to analyze query performance metrics such as:

- Query latency

- Query throughput

- Query CPU usage

You can filter and explore performance by DML type, time, or application.

Monitoring with CloudWatch

Amazon DocumentDB automatically emits metrics to Amazon CloudWatch. Key metrics include:

- DatabaseConnections

- ReadThroughput, WriteThroughput

- InsertLatency, UpdateLatency

- LowMemNumOperationsThrottled (throttled ops)

- ReplicationLag (for replicas)

Set up CloudWatch alarms for thresholds to alert on unusual patterns.

Integrating Audit and Monitoring Tools

You can extend monitoring using:

- **Amazon OpenSearch** (via change streams and pipeline integration)

- **Amazon S3** for long-term log storage

- **Amazon EventBridge** to trigger alerts on specific operations

---

Summary

Auditing and monitoring in Amazon DocumentDB provide full visibility into who is accessing your data, when, and how. The combination of **audit logs**, **CloudTrail**, **CloudWatch**, and **profiler tools** ensures:

- Comprehensive DML visibility

- Historical and real-time access tracking

- Compliance with data governance policies

Key Recommendations:

- Enable audit logs and filter categories to reduce overhead

- Integrate with CloudTrail for full API auditability

- Use Profiler to detect slow or misbehaving queries

- Monitor key CloudWatch metrics and use alarms

- Export logs to S3 for compliance and retention

Part VII – Operations and Maintenance

Chapter 22: Backup and Restore

Snapshots and PITR (Point-in-Time Restore)

Reliable backup and restore capabilities are essential for protecting data against accidental deletion, corruption, or failure scenarios. Amazon DocumentDB offers two primary mechanisms for safeguarding your data: **manual snapshots** and **point-in-time restore (PITR)**. Both leverage the robust underlying storage infrastructure that replicates data across multiple Availability Zones (AZs), ensuring durability and availability.

This chapter explores the concepts, features, and best practices of backup and restore in Amazon DocumentDB, focusing on **snapshots** and **PITR**, and guiding you through how to plan, configure, and use these capabilities effectively.

Introduction to Backup and Restore in Amazon DocumentDB

Amazon DocumentDB provides **continuous, incremental backups** by default. These backups enable point-in-time restore and do not impact database performance or availability. Additionally, users can create **manual cluster snapshots** on-demand, which serve as restorable backups that persist beyond the automatic backup retention window.

Amazon DocumentDB uses **Amazon S3** as the underlying backup storage system, designed for **11 9s (99.999999999%) durability**. Backups are **storage-efficient**, and because they are **incremental**, you're only charged for the differences between backups.

Snapshots

Snapshots in Amazon DocumentDB are full backups of your cluster at a specific moment in time. They are stored in Amazon S3 and can be retained indefinitely, unlike automatic backups that expire after a defined retention period.

Types of Snapshots

1. **Automated Snapshots**

    - Created automatically as part of PITR (discussed later).

    - Managed by AWS based on your defined **retention window** (1 to 35 days).

    - Not user-visible as snapshot resources in the console or CLI.

2. **Manual Snapshots**

- Explicitly created by users.

- Persist until manually deleted.

- Ideal for long-term archiving, versioning, and milestone backups (e.g., pre-deployment).

Creating a Manual Snapshot

Snapshots can be created using:

- **AWS Management Console**

- **AWS CLI**

- **Amazon DocumentDB API**

Example (AWS CLI):

```
aws docdb create-db-cluster-snapshot \
   --db-cluster-snapshot-identifier my-snapshot-2025-01-01 \
   --db-cluster-identifier my-cluster
```

Snapshot Storage

- Snapshot data is stored **separately** from the live database.

- Snapshot creation is **instantaneous**, as it uses **storage-level pointers**.

- Snapshots do **not impact performance** of the cluster during creation.

Managing Snapshots

You can:

- **List** existing snapshots

- **Tag** snapshots for billing and management

- **Copy** snapshots across Regions

- **Restore** a new cluster from a snapshot

- **Share** encrypted snapshots with other AWS accounts

Copying Snapshots Across Regions

Amazon DocumentDB allows you to copy manual snapshots to another AWS Region for **disaster recovery** or **regional expansion**.

Key considerations:

- **Encryption settings** must be compatible.

- Snapshot copying can take several minutes depending on size.

aws docdb copy-db-cluster-snapshot \

```
  --source-db-cluster-snapshot-identifier arn:aws:rds:us-
west-1:123456789012:snapshot:my-snapshot \
  --target-db-cluster-snapshot-identifier my-snapshot-copy
\
  --source-region us-west-1
```

Sharing Snapshots

- You can share unencrypted snapshots with other AWS accounts.

- To share encrypted snapshots, both accounts must use the **same AWS KMS key**, or the key must be shared.

Point-in-Time Restore (PITR)

Point-in-time restore allows you to restore your cluster to **any second within your backup retention window**, up to the most recent 5 minutes. This is extremely useful in recovering from:

- Accidental data deletion

- Schema changes gone wrong

- Corruption due to application bugs

How PITR Works

- Amazon DocumentDB **continuously backs up** your data.

- PITR works by replaying changes from the backup window to a specific point in time.

- The system maintains **incremental backups**, so restoration is fast and storage-efficient.

Backup Retention Period

- You can set the **retention window** from **1 to 35 days**.

- This applies to **automated backups**, which are used for PITR.

- Retention settings can be updated at any time:

```
aws docdb modify-db-cluster \
  --db-cluster-identifier my-cluster \
  --backup-retention-period 14
```

Performing a PITR Operation

When you perform a PITR:

- A **new cluster** is created.

- You must **specify the target timestamp** in UTC.

- PITR does not overwrite existing clusters.

Example (AWS CLI):

```
aws docdb restore-db-cluster-to-point-in-time \
  --source-db-cluster-identifier my-cluster \
  --target-db-cluster-identifier my-cluster-restored \
  --restore-to-time 2025-03-26T13:00:00Z
```

PITR Considerations

- You can restore to any point in time **within the retention period**.

- Restoration is **transactionally consistent** to the chosen second.

- PITR does **not restore manual or shared snapshots**—only automated backups.

Backup Storage and Costs

Backup storage is billed based on:

- The total volume of **backup data** retained (automated + snapshots).

- Charges begin **after** the allocated **free backup storage** (equal to the size of your cluster).

Key considerations:

- **Automated backups** are free up to the size of your cluster.

- **Snapshots** incur additional storage charges.

- Deleted clusters retain automated backups **until the retention period expires** or the cluster is manually deleted with --skip-final-snapshot.

Comparing PITR vs. Snapshots

Feature	Manual Snapshots	Point-in-Time Restore (PITR)
Initiated By	User	System (continuous)
Restore Target	Specific snapshot timestamp	Any second within retention window
Retention	Indefinite (user-defined)	1–35 days (configurable)
Storage Cost	Paid per GiB-month	Free up to cluster size
Use Case	Long-term archiving	Rapid recovery
Impact on Performance	None	None
Restores to New Cluster	✓	✓

Best Practices

1. **Enable Backups on All Production Clusters**

   o Never run production workloads with a backup retention period of 0.

2. **Create Manual Snapshots Before Major Changes**

    o   Useful for rollbacks during schema migrations or application deployments.

3. **Use PITR for Short-Term Recovery**

    o   Restore to a precise point before data corruption or deletion.

4. **Automate Snapshot Management**

    o   Use AWS Backup or custom scripts to schedule snapshots, rotate old ones, and tag resources.

5. **Test Restores Regularly**

    o   Ensure that restore operations work as expected by periodically testing snapshot or PITR recovery.

6. **Use KMS for Encryption**

    o   All snapshots and PITR backups are encrypted if the source cluster is encrypted.

7. **Monitor with CloudWatch**

    o   Use metrics like BackupStorageUsed to monitor trends and set cost alerts.

Common CLI Commands

Operation	AWS CLI Command
Create manual snapshot	create-db-cluster-snapshot
Restore from snapshot	restore-db-cluster-from-snapshot
Restore to point in time	restore-db-cluster-to-point-in-time
Copy snapshot	copy-db-cluster-snapshot
Delete snapshot	delete-db-cluster-snapshot
Modify backup retention period	modify-db-cluster
List snapshots	describe-db-cluster-snapshots

Security and Compliance Considerations

- **Encryption**

    - All backups are encrypted at rest using
      AWS KMS keys.

    - Encrypted clusters require encryption on all
      associated backups and snapshots.

- **Access Control**

    - Use IAM policies to control who can view,
      create, or delete snapshots.

    - Example IAM permissions:

        - rds:CreateDBClusterSnapshot

        - rds:DeleteDBClusterSnapshot

- rds:RestoreDBClusterFromSnapshot

- **Auditing**

    - Use **AWS CloudTrail** to log snapshot-related API calls for auditing and compliance.

Summary

Amazon DocumentDB's backup and restore mechanisms are critical components of a resilient database architecture.

Key capabilities include:

- **Manual snapshots** for persistent, on-demand backups.

- **Point-in-time restore (PITR)** for granular recovery within a defined retention window.

- Highly durable backups stored in Amazon S3, with no impact on performance.

- Simple CLI/API-based operations to automate backup and recovery.

- Full encryption support and Region-to-Region snapshot replication.

By implementing robust backup policies and understanding the available recovery tools, you can ensure that your Amazon DocumentDB workloads are protected from data loss and operational disruptions.

Chapter 23: Maintenance and Patching

Maintaining a healthy and secure Amazon DocumentDB environment is essential for ensuring availability, performance, and compliance. Maintenance and patching in Amazon DocumentDB are fully managed by AWS, allowing users to focus on application development while Amazon handles underlying infrastructure updates, including database engine versioning and operating system patches.

This chapter explains how Amazon DocumentDB handles engine version management and OS-level maintenance, and how you can control and monitor these updates.

Engine Versioning

Amazon DocumentDB supports multiple versions of the MongoDB-compatible database engine. As with any managed database service, AWS periodically releases **engine updates** that provide:

- New features

- Performance improvements

- Security enhancements

- Bug fixes

These updates may involve **minor version patches** or **major version upgrades**, depending on the nature of the release.

Types of Engine Version Updates

1. **Minor Version Patches**

   - Typically backward-compatible

   - Focus on bug fixes, performance enhancements, and minor features

   - Applied during the defined maintenance window

   - Do **not require application code changes**

2. **Major Version Upgrades**

   - Introduce significant functional changes

   - May include breaking changes

   - Require **manual intervention and planning**

   - AWS does not automatically apply major upgrades

Major upgrades include transitions such as:

- MongoDB 3.6 → 4.0

- MongoDB 4.0 → 5.0

You can verify supported versions and functional differences in the **Amazon DocumentDB Developer Guide**.

Viewing the Current Engine Version

You can view the current engine version of your cluster using the AWS Management Console or AWS CLI.

Console:

1. Navigate to the **Amazon DocumentDB** console.

2. Click on your **cluster name**.

3. The **engine version** is listed in the "Cluster details" section.

CLI:

```
aws docdb describe-db-clusters --query
"DBClusters[*].EngineVersion"
```

Managing Version Updates

Amazon DocumentDB separates major and minor updates to give users control over version transitions.

- **Minor updates** are applied automatically during the **maintenance window**, which you can customize.

- **Major upgrades** must be initiated manually. AWS provides tooling and guidance to test and apply these safely.

To manage engine versions:

- Use **cloned clusters** for testing new versions.

- Schedule upgrades during periods of **low usage**.

- **Monitor application behavior** after upgrades for any compatibility issues.

Best Practices for Engine Versioning

- **Test before upgrading**: Clone your cluster and perform application-level validation against the new version.

- **Review release notes**: Read the AWS release notes to understand changes.

- **Monitor post-upgrade**: Use CloudWatch metrics and application logs to track performance or error trends.

- **Automate alerts**: Set up notifications for available updates using CloudWatch Events or AWS Config.

OS Updates and Patches

Amazon DocumentDB runs on AWS-managed infrastructure, which includes the underlying **operating system** (OS). While you don't have direct access to the OS layer, AWS handles OS updates as part of the fully managed service.

These updates may include:

- Kernel patches

- Security updates

- Performance fixes

OS Update Scheduling

Operating system updates are applied during the **preferred maintenance window** you define for your cluster. These updates are designed to be **non-intrusive**, with minimal impact on running workloads.

However, in rare cases, patches may require:

- **Restarting instances** (leading to a short service disruption)

- **Failovers** to replicas in multi-AZ deployments

Tip: Always deploy at least one read replica in a different Availability Zone to reduce downtime risks during patching.

Viewing and Modifying the Maintenance Window

You can configure the preferred maintenance window to specify when AWS may apply patches.

Console:

1. Go to the Amazon DocumentDB Console.

2. Choose your cluster.

3. Select **Modify**.

4. Under **Maintenance window**, choose the desired day and time.

CLI:

```
aws docdb modify-db-cluster \
  --db-cluster-identifier your-cluster-id \
  --preferred-maintenance-window "sun:05:00-sun:06:00"
```

Monitoring OS-Level Updates

While OS updates are largely transparent, you can still monitor for changes using:

- **Event Subscriptions**: Subscribe to maintenance events via SNS.

- **CloudWatch Logs**: Track instance status metrics like CPU, memory, and uptime.

- **Cluster Logs**: Use performance insights to detect any post-update anomalies.

Impact and Failover Behavior

When an OS patch necessitates a reboot:

- The **primary instance** may undergo a failover.

- One of the **read replicas** is promoted to primary, if available.

- The affected instance is restarted and resumes after patching.

This behavior ensures **high availability**, especially for production environments with multiple instances.

Recommended Practices for OS Patching

- **Stagger your maintenance windows** across clusters if you operate multiple environments (e.g., dev, staging, prod).

- Use **CloudWatch alarms** to detect anomalies following OS patches.

- Keep **read replicas** in separate AZs to avoid a single point of failure.

- Regularly review your **event logs** to stay informed about system-level changes.

Engine Patch Notifications

Amazon DocumentDB provides automated notifications for upcoming engine and OS maintenance activities. These notifications include:

- Scheduled maintenance windows

- Type of maintenance (e.g., OS update, engine patch)

- Expected impact (e.g., reboot required)

How to Receive Notifications:

1. **Enable Event Subscriptions**:

    - Use the Amazon DocumentDB console or CLI to subscribe to maintenance events.

    - Configure notifications through **Amazon SNS** topics.

2. **Event Categories** include:

    - pending-maintenance

    - maintenance-start

    - maintenance-complete

CLI Example to Create a Subscription:

```
aws docdb create-event-subscription \
  --subscription-name patch-alerts \
  --sns-topic-arn arn:aws:sns:us-east-
1:123456789012:MySNSTopic \
  --source-type db-instance \
  --event-categories maintenance
```

Managing Maintenance with Minimal Disruption

To maintain service reliability during maintenance:

- **Use multi-AZ deployments**: Enables failover to replicas during patching.

- **Schedule during low-traffic hours**: Align your maintenance window with off-peak periods.

- **Automate backups**: Ensure you have up-to-date snapshots before major updates.

- **Monitor with CloudWatch and CloudTrail**: Detect unexpected behavior early.

Summary

Amazon DocumentDB handles the heavy lifting of database and OS maintenance for you, but gives you control over **when** and **how** those updates are applied. By understanding how engine versioning and OS patching work, and by leveraging AWS tools for monitoring and automation, you can ensure your clusters remain secure, performant, and highly available — with minimal manual intervention.

Chapter 24: Monitoring and Performance Insights

Performance Metrics, CloudWatch Dashboards

Introduction

In cloud-native applications, observability is not optional—it's a foundational requirement for ensuring availability, scalability, and performance. Amazon DocumentDB provides comprehensive monitoring capabilities through **performance metrics**, **CloudWatch integration**, and **Performance Insights**, enabling developers, DBAs, and DevOps engineers to understand and optimize workload behavior.

This chapter explores the core tools and techniques available to monitor Amazon DocumentDB performance, focusing on key metrics, CloudWatch dashboards, and the Amazon Performance Insights feature. With these tools, you can proactively diagnose bottlenecks, fine-tune your application, and ensure that your database continues to meet your business needs.

Performance Metrics in Amazon DocumentDB

Amazon DocumentDB automatically collects a wide range of performance and resource utilization metrics. These are exposed via **Amazon CloudWatch** and can be visualized, analyzed, and alarmed against in near real-time.

Types of Metrics

Amazon DocumentDB emits metrics at both the **cluster level** and **instance level**, categorized into several key groups:

1. **CPU and Memory**

   - CPUUtilization: Percentage of compute capacity used.

   - FreeableMemory: Unused memory, helpful to detect memory pressure.

2. **Storage and I/O**

   - VolumeBytesUsed: Size of the storage volume in bytes.

   - ReadIOPS / WriteIOPS: I/O operations per second.

   - ReadThroughput / WriteThroughput: Throughput in bytes/second.

3. **Connections and Requests**

   - DatabaseConnections: Number of active client connections.

   - Latency: End-to-end request latency.

   - NetworkThroughput: Inbound/outbound network traffic in bytes/second.

4. **Availability and Reliability**

  o ReplicaLag: Time delay (in milliseconds) for replicas to sync with the primary.

  o LowMemThrottleQueueDepth: Indicates throttling due to low memory.

  o Deadlocks: Number of transaction deadlocks.

5. **Throttling and Limits**

  o ThrottleEvents: Number of events where requests were throttled.

  o SwapUsage: Swap file usage, often a symptom of memory pressure.

Instance-Specific vs. Cluster Metrics

- **Cluster Metrics**: Offer a macro-level view—helpful for capacity planning and workload analysis.

- **Instance Metrics**: Useful for granular diagnosis, particularly for identifying hotspots or resource contention on a specific instance.

Custom Metrics

Although Amazon DocumentDB does not support user-defined custom metrics directly, you can push application-level metrics (e.g., query response time, cache hit ratio) to CloudWatch using the PutMetricData API.

Using CloudWatch for Monitoring

Amazon CloudWatch is the central monitoring platform for AWS services, and is fully integrated with DocumentDB. It provides:

- Metric visualization via charts and dashboards

- Alarm configuration and SNS notifications

- Event correlation and logging (via CloudTrail and logs)

- Long-term retention and metric history

Accessing CloudWatch Metrics

To view metrics:

1. Open the **CloudWatch Console**.

2. Navigate to **Metrics** > **Browse**.

3. Select **DocDB** > choose from:

   o Per-Instance Metrics

   o Per-Cluster Metrics

- ○ Performance Insights (if enabled)

Example Metrics View

Here's a basic metric dashboard for an instance:

- **CPUUtilization** over time

- **ReplicaLag** spikes indicating replication delays

- **DatabaseConnections** trending upward

- **WriteThroughput** increasing during batch jobs

Creating Alarms

CloudWatch lets you set alarms to notify you when a metric crosses a threshold. For example:

If ReplicaLag > 500ms for 2 consecutive datapoints → send SNS alert

Alarm use cases:

- High CPU → Scale up or investigate queries

- High latency → Trigger automated failover

- Low memory → Prevent instance crashes

Performance Insights for Amazon DocumentDB

Performance Insights is an advanced monitoring tool that provides query-level visibility into your Amazon DocumentDB workload. It helps you identify slow-running operations, blocked queries, and bottlenecks.

Enabling Performance Insights

To enable:

1. Go to the **Amazon DocumentDB Console**.

2. Choose your cluster.

3. Modify the cluster and enable **Performance Insights**.

4. Select a retention period (default is 7 days, extendable to 2 years).

5. Save changes and reboot if prompted.

Alternatively, use the AWS CLI:

```
aws docdb modify-db-cluster \
  --db-cluster-identifier my-cluster \
  --enable-performance-insights \
  --performance-insights-retention-period 7
```

Performance Insights Dashboard

265

Once enabled, the dashboard shows:

- **Database Load**: Active sessions over time

- **Top Queries**: Sorted by CPU, I/O, latency

- **Wait Events**: Blocking, I/O contention, lock waits

- **Query Execution Plans**

You can filter by time, dimension (user, host, application), and view historical performance trends.

Use Cases

- Identify high-latency queries

- Spot inefficient aggregation or filter logic

- Detect locking or concurrency issues

- Tune indexing strategy

CloudWatch Dashboards

CloudWatch Dashboards allow you to build custom visualizations using one or more widgets to monitor your Amazon DocumentDB environment at a glance.

Creating a Dashboard

1. In the **CloudWatch Console**, go to **Dashboards**.

2. Click **Create Dashboard**, name it (e.g., DocDB-Monitoring).

3. Add widgets:

   o Line charts for CPUUtilization, WriteIOPS, ReplicaLag

   o Number widgets for active connections

   o Heat maps or stacked graphs to compare instance metrics

Example Widget Setup

Metric	Widget Type	Notes
CPUUtilization	Line	Monitors CPU saturation
ReplicaLag	Line	Helps track read consistency
FreeableMemory	Line	Indicates memory pressure
DatabaseConnections	Number	Active user load
Read/Write Throughput	Line	Application activity monitor

Refresh and Sharing

- Dashboards refresh every 1–5 minutes.

- You can share dashboards via URL or integrate them into **CloudWatch Synthetics**, **Lambda**, or third-party tools.

Best Practices for Monitoring

- **Set CloudWatch alarms** on critical metrics (CPU, memory, lag).

- **Use Performance Insights** for query tuning and execution plan analysis.

- **Monitor trend changes** using CloudWatch metrics over days/weeks.

- **Enable detailed monitoring** for shorter polling intervals.

- **Integrate with AWS Chatbot or SNS** for real-time alerts into Slack, email, or SMS.

- **Automate scaling** based on metric thresholds using Lambda or EventBridge.

Sample Troubleshooting Scenarios

1. High Replica Lag

- Check write volume on primary.

- Review IOPS metrics.

- Consider increasing read instance class.

2. Increasing CPU Utilization

- Use Performance Insights to detect query bottlenecks.

- Optimize queries or add indexes.

- Consider scaling up to a larger instance.

3. Frequent Throttling

- Investigate memory-related metrics (LowMemThrottleQueueDepth).

- Upgrade instance or distribute load.

4. Application Errors

- Correlate error spikes with CloudWatch logs and metrics.

- Use Deadlocks, SwapUsage, and NetworkThroughput as diagnostic clues.

Summary

Amazon DocumentDB delivers powerful observability tools for both high-level infrastructure monitoring and deep workload inspection. With CloudWatch and Performance Insights, you can detect problems early, drill into root causes, and make informed optimization decisions.

Whether you're running small test environments or mission-critical workloads, effective use of these monitoring tools ensures high availability, minimal latency, and consistent performance for your document database applications.

Chapter 25: Managing Resources

Efficient resource management is vital to running scalable, secure, and cost-effective Amazon DocumentDB environments. Amazon DocumentDB provides a set of tools that allow developers and administrators to organize, control, and customize how clusters and instances behave. This chapter will explore how to manage **Subnet Groups**, **Tags**, **Parameter Groups**, and **Amazon Resource Names (ARNs)** — foundational concepts for controlling networking, configuration, and resource identification in DocumentDB deployments.

Subnet Groups, Tags

Amazon DocumentDB requires networking configuration to define how and where resources are deployed. Subnet Groups and Tags are key features that help in organizing and isolating workloads effectively.

Subnet Groups

A **subnet group** is a collection of Amazon VPC subnets that defines the network boundaries for your Amazon DocumentDB cluster. When you create a cluster, you must specify a subnet group. DocumentDB then places instances within the subnets in that group.

Purpose of Subnet Groups

- Ensure cluster instances are launched in **specific Availability Zones**

- Define **network isolation** and **IP address ranges**

- Control **connectivity and routing** to and from the cluster

Creating a Subnet Group

You can create a subnet group using the **AWS Management Console**, **AWS CLI**, or **AWS SDKs**.

Example CLI command to create a subnet group

```
aws docdb create-db-subnet-group \
   --db-subnet-group-name my-subnet-group \
   --db-subnet-group-description "My DocumentDB subnet group" \
   --subnet-ids subnet-abc123 subnet-def456
```

Best Practices

- Include **subnets in at least two Availability Zones** for high availability.

271

- Associate **private subnets** if your cluster doesn't need public internet access.

- Use **security groups** in conjunction to control access at the network level.

Tags

Tags are metadata labels assigned to AWS resources. They consist of **key-value pairs** and are used to organize, identify, and manage DocumentDB resources.

Common Use Cases for Tags

- **Cost allocation**: Assign tags for departments, environments, or projects.

- **Automation**: Identify resources for lifecycle operations (e.g., backups or cleanup).

- **Security and compliance**: Mark resources with compliance tags for audits.

Example tag

Key: Environment
Value: Production

Managing Tags

You can **add, update, or delete** tags using the AWS Console or CLI.

CLI Example: Tagging a Cluster

```
aws docdb add-tags-to-resource \
    --resource-name arn:aws:rds:us-east-
1:123456789012:cluster:my-cluster \
    --tags Key=Project,Value=CRM
Key=Team,Value=DevOps
```

Tag Constraints

- Maximum of **50 tags** per resource.

- Tag keys must be **unique per resource**.

- Keys and values are case sensitive.

Best Practices

- Establish **tagging conventions** across your organization.

- Automate tagging via **infrastructure-as-code (IaC)** templates.

- Regularly audit and clean up unused or outdated tags.

Parameter Groups

Amazon DocumentDB uses **cluster parameter groups** to manage configuration settings that control the behavior of your cluster. These parameters include memory usage thresholds, diagnostic logging, TTL options, and more.

Understanding Parameter Groups

Each cluster is associated with exactly one **cluster parameter group**. This group defines how the DocumentDB engine behaves.

- Changes to a parameter group affect **all instances** in the associated cluster.

- You can use **default** parameter groups or create **custom** ones.

Default vs. Custom Parameter Groups

Type	Editable	Use Case
Default	No	Quick setups, general use
Custom	Yes	Fine-tuned configurations

Creating and Using a Parameter Group

CLI Example: Create Parameter Group

```
aws docdb create-db-cluster-parameter-group \
  --db-cluster-parameter-group-name my-params \
  --db-parameter-group-family docdb5.0 \
  --description "Custom settings for production"
```

Modifying a parameter:

```
aws docdb modify-db-cluster-parameter-group \
  --db-cluster-parameter-group-name my-params \
  --parameters
"ParameterName=ttl_monitor_enabled,ParameterValue=tr
ue,ApplyMethod=immediate"
```

Applying the Parameter Group

You must **modify your cluster** to use the new parameter group:

```
aws docdb modify-db-cluster \
  --db-cluster-identifier my-cluster \
  --db-cluster-parameter-group-name my-params
```

Changes are typically applied **immediately**, but some may require a **cluster reboot**.

Parameter Group Best Practices

- Use **custom parameter groups** for environment-specific settings (e.g., dev, test, prod).

- Group **related parameter changes** into a single parameter group.

- Regularly **review and document** parameter changes for compliance and troubleshooting.

Common Parameters

Parameter Name	Description	Default
ttl_monitor_enabled	Enables TTL deletion	false
audit_logs	Enables audit logging	disabled
profiler_enabled	Enables operation profiling	false
max_connections	Max number of concurrent client connections	Varies

ARNs (Amazon Resource Names)

Amazon Resource Names (ARNs) uniquely identify AWS resources across all services, including Amazon DocumentDB. Understanding ARNs is critical for managing access, automation, and integrations.

What is an ARN?

An **ARN** is a standardized string that represents a specific resource in AWS. Its general format is:

arn:partition:service:region:account-id:resource

ARN Format for DocumentDB

Resource Type	Example ARN
Cluster	arn:aws:rds:us-east-1:123456789012:cluster:my-cluster
Instance	arn:aws:rds:us-east-1:123456789012:db:my-instance
Subnet Group	arn:aws:rds:us-east-1:123456789012:subgrp:my-subnet-group

Use Cases for ARNs

- **IAM Policies**: Grant or deny access to DocumentDB resources.

- **CloudFormation**: Reference specific clusters or subnet groups.

- **Tagging and Logging**: Associate events or logs with specific resources.

Finding ARNs

You can retrieve ARNs via:

- **AWS Management Console** (under resource details)

- **AWS CLI**

```
aws docdb describe-db-clusters \
  --query "DBClusters[*].DBClusterArn"
```

Tips for Working with ARNs

- Use **wildcards** in IAM policies to grant access to all resources of a type.

- Match exact ARNs for **least-privilege** permissions.

- Validate ARNs before using them in automation scripts or Lambda functions.

Summary

Resource management in Amazon DocumentDB is a foundational skill for architects and DevOps engineers. By mastering:

- **Subnet Groups** to define your network boundaries,

- **Tags** to organize and automate resource tracking,

- **Parameter Groups** to fine-tune engine behavior,

- and **ARNs** to securely and precisely reference resources,

you can ensure your DocumentDB infrastructure is secure, scalable, and maintainable. Proper governance and operational consistency are essential as your clusters grow and become critical components of your cloud architecture.

Part VIII – Migrations and Upgrades

Chapter 26: Migrating to DocumentDB

Migrating your data and applications from MongoDB to Amazon DocumentDB requires careful planning and execution to ensure a smooth, reliable transition. Whether you're moving from an on-premises deployment, self-managed cloud instance, or another database service, Amazon DocumentDB provides a range of **migration tools** and **strategies** to match your technical needs and downtime tolerance.

This chapter covers:

- The most commonly used migration tools such as **AWS Database Migration Service (DMS)** and **MongoDB native utilities** like mongodump/mongorestore

- Three core migration approaches: **Offline**, **Online**, and **Hybrid**

- Key steps, best practices, and considerations for each method

---

Tools for Migrating to DocumentDB

Amazon DocumentDB supports several tools and utilities to facilitate migration. Choosing the right tool depends on your data volume, availability needs, and operational constraints.

AWS Database Migration Service (DMS)

AWS DMS is a powerful, fully managed service that can perform both full loads and ongoing replication from a MongoDB source to Amazon DocumentDB.

Key Capabilities:

- **Full Load**: Copies existing collections and documents.

- **Change Data Capture (CDC)**: Replicates new changes in real time using **MongoDB change streams**.

- **Minimal Downtime**: Enables near-zero-downtime migrations.

- **Monitoring**: Provides detailed task logs and CloudWatch metrics.

Requirements:

- Source MongoDB must be **replica set-enabled**.

- Change streams must be **enabled** and **retention duration** configured.

- AWS DMS requires:

  - **Replication instance**

  - **Source and target endpoints**

○ **Migration task definition**

Tip: Use DMS for live production migrations where availability is critical.

MongoDB Native Tools

mongodump **and** mongorestore

These CLI tools are suitable for **offline migrations**, development environments, or lower-volume production workloads.

- mongodump: Exports MongoDB collections to a binary .bson format.

- mongorestore: Imports .bson files into Amazon DocumentDB.

Advantages:

- Simple, fast for smaller datasets

- Supports namespace filtering (e.g., only specific databases or collections)

- Flexible for scripting or automation

Limitations:

- Not suitable for live replication

- No built-in support for CDC

- Requires manual downtime coordination

Other Utilities

- mongoexport / mongoimport: Use for JSON or CSV exports; slower than mongodump for large datasets.

- **Third-party ETL tools**: Tools like Talend, StreamSets, or custom AWS Glue jobs can be integrated for specific use cases or transformations during migration.

Migration Methods

Amazon DocumentDB supports three primary migration strategies: **Offline**, **Online**, and **Hybrid**. Each offers tradeoffs between simplicity, complexity, downtime, and cost.

Offline Migration

Offline migration is the most straightforward approach, but it requires a downtime window.

When to Use:

- Application can tolerate temporary downtime

- Small to medium-sized datasets

- Simpler operational environments (e.g., non-prod or test systems)

Step-by-Step:

1. **Stop application writes** to the source MongoDB.

Export data using mongodump:

```
mongodump --
uri="mongodb://<user>:<password>@source-host:27017" -
-out=/data/dump
```

2. **Create Amazon DocumentDB cluster** and connect using TLS.

Import data using mongorestore:

```
mongorestore --host=<docdb-endpoint> --ssl --
username=<user> --password=<password> /data/dump
```

3. **Recreate indexes** manually or using automation scripts.

4. **Validate data** and restart application pointing to Amazon DocumentDB.

Advantages:

- Simplicity

- No external services required

- Complete control over the process

Disadvantages:

- Application downtime during migration

- Manual effort for validation and index recreation

- Longer cutover window for large datasets

Online Migration

Online migration minimizes or eliminates downtime by **replicating changes in real time** using AWS DMS.

When to Use:

- Production workloads

- High data volumes

- Minimal acceptable downtime (e.g., seconds or minutes)

Architecture Overview:

```
[ MongoDB Source ] ---> (Full Load) ---> [ Amazon DocumentDB ]
       |                      ↑
  (Change Streams) -------> (Ongoing Replication via DMS)
```

Step-by-Step:

1. **Prepare MongoDB source**:

   ○ Must be a replica set

   ○ Enable change streams

   ○ Set changeStreamOptions.retentionDurationHours in the cluster parameter group

2. **Create Amazon DocumentDB cluster**

3. **Use AWS DMS to perform full load**:

   ○ Create a **replication instance**

   ○ Configure **source and target endpoints**

   ○ Define and run **full load + CDC** migration task

4. **Monitor replication status** in DMS console or via CloudWatch

5. **Wait for lag to reach zero**, then cut over application to DocumentDB

Advantages:

- Near-zero downtime

- Scalable for large datasets

- Monitoring and logging built-in

Disadvantages:

- More complex setup

- Requires AWS IAM roles and permissions

- Change stream and DMS configuration must be precise

  Best Practice: Perform test migrations with production-sized datasets before executing final cutover.

Hybrid Migration

Hybrid migration combines offline and online methods. It offers more flexibility in certain scenarios, such as:

- Migrating critical collections live while others are migrated offline

- Performing the majority of data transfer offline, then syncing changes with a custom script or tool

When to Use:

- Legacy environments or partial migration

- Limited access to DMS

- Teams with custom sync pipelines

Example Strategy:

1. Use mongodump for static or historical collections.

2. Use a change-capture tool (e.g., DMS or custom Lambda functions) to track and replicate ongoing writes.

3. Merge both stages during cutover, ensuring consistency.

Advantages:

- Flexible

- Balances downtime and complexity

- Allows staging of data ahead of time

Disadvantages:

- More complex reconciliation

- Potential consistency issues without strict coordination

Testing and Validation

Regardless of the method, rigorous testing is essential.

- **Data validation**: Use document counts, checksums, or hash comparison tools.

- **Application testing**: Validate queries, transactions, and schema mappings.

- **Performance testing**: Monitor replica lag, query times, and index behavior in DocumentDB.

- **Failover simulation**: Test resiliency of the target cluster.

Best Practices

- Use **TLS encryption** for all migrations to protect data in transit.

- Monitor **I/O operations** to avoid billing surprises during large migrations.

- **Index early**: Missing indexes can cause degraded performance post-migration.

- For **DMS**, consider using **multi-threaded full load** with parallelism for faster migrations.

- Run **post-migration analytics** to verify DocumentDB behavior matches MongoDB.

Summary

Amazon DocumentDB offers a robust and flexible migration ecosystem that accommodates a wide range of workloads and operational constraints. Whether you're migrating a production workload or a development database, the combination of tools like **AWS DMS**, **mongodump**, and **custom strategies** enables safe and efficient transitions.

Strategy	Tools Used	Downtime	Complexity	Best For
Offline	mongodump/ mongorestore	High	Low	Dev/Test, Small Workloads
Online	AWS DMS	Low	High	Production, Real-time Sync
Hybrid	Both + Custom Pipelines	Medium	Medium	Partial Migrations, Legacy

Chapter 27: Engine Upgrades

MVU Process
Best Practices and Troubleshooting

Introduction

As Amazon DocumentDB continues to evolve with new features, security patches, and performance improvements, keeping your cluster up to date becomes essential. Amazon DocumentDB supports **in-place major version upgrades (MVUs)**, allowing you to upgrade from older versions like 3.6 or 4.0 to the latest supported version such as 5.0.

This chapter explores the **MVU process**, outlines **best practices** for planning and executing upgrades, and provides **troubleshooting guidance** to help mitigate risks and minimize downtime during your upgrade path.

Understanding Engine Versions in Amazon DocumentDB

Amazon DocumentDB is compatible with multiple versions of MongoDB, such as:

- MongoDB 3.6 (legacy support)

- MongoDB 4.0

- MongoDB 5.0 (latest supported)

Newer versions introduce features such as:

- JSON schema validation

- Vector search

- Improved transaction support

- Enhanced compatibility and performance

Upgrading enables access to these innovations and ensures long-term support from AWS.

What Is a Major Version Upgrade (MVU)?

A **major version upgrade (MVU)** updates your Amazon DocumentDB cluster to a **new engine version**, for example:

From: Amazon DocumentDB 4.0
To: Amazon DocumentDB 5.0

Unlike patch updates (which may be applied automatically), MVUs are **manual operations**. They involve restarting the cluster and modifying its internal components to align with the new engine version.

MVU Process Overview

The MVU process consists of the following key phases:

1. **Preparation and Validation**

2. **Testing via Cloned Cluster**

3. **Initiating the Upgrade**

4. **Monitoring the Upgrade Progress**

5. **Post-Upgrade Validation**

Each phase is crucial to ensuring a successful and low-risk upgrade.

Phase 1: Preparation and Validation

Before initiating an upgrade, review the following:

- **Current engine version**: Identify whether your cluster is eligible (e.g., only 3.6 → 5.0 or 4.0 → 5.0).

- **Functional differences**: Review the release notes and functional differences between versions.

- **Unsupported features**: Confirm if any deprecated commands or data types exist in your current workload.

- **Cluster health**: Ensure the cluster is **healthy**, with **no ongoing backups or failovers**.

Checklist

- ✅ Back up your cluster (snapshot).

- ✅ Review release notes and breaking changes.

- ✅ Confirm workload compatibility.

- ✅ Inform stakeholders of maintenance windows.

- ✅ Ensure sufficient capacity for replicas and failover.

Phase 2: Test Using a Cloned Cluster

Before performing the MVU on a production cluster, **test the upgrade on a clone**.

Steps

1. Create a **clone** of your current cluster.

2. Upgrade the cloned cluster to the target version (e.g., 5.0).

3. Run **functional and performance tests** on your application.

4. Validate compatibility of drivers, queries, and integrations.

Benefits

- Risk-free environment for validating workloads.

- Can benchmark performance under real data conditions.

- Ideal for **CI/CD pipelines** or dev environments.

Phase 3: Initiating the MVU

Once testing is complete, you can begin the upgrade on the live cluster.

Initiation Methods

- **AWS Management Console**:
  Navigate to the cluster, choose **Modify**, and select the new engine version under **Engine version**.

- **AWS CLI**:

```
aws docdb modify-db-cluster \
  --db-cluster-identifier my-cluster \
```

```
--engine-version 5.0.0 \
--apply-immediately
```

- **CloudFormation**: Update engine version in your stack template.

Note

- MVU **restarts the entire cluster**, causing a **brief service interruption**.

- It may take **several minutes** depending on cluster size and workload.

Phase 4: Monitoring the Upgrade

You can monitor the upgrade using:

- **Amazon CloudWatch**:

  - EngineUptime

  - ClusterStatus

  - InstanceStatus

- **Console Events**:

  - View recent events for upgrade start/completion/failure.

- **API**:

  - describe-db-clusters to check EngineVersion and Status.

Expected Downtime

- The cluster is briefly unavailable during the restart phase.

- Typically between **2 to 10 minutes**, depending on instance class and replica count.

Phase 5: Post-Upgrade Validation

After the upgrade completes:

- Test application **read/write operations**.

- Verify **replica lag** (should be low or zero).

- Confirm CloudWatch **error metrics** show no anomalies.

- Validate functionality of **transactions**, **queries**, and **drivers**.

Recommended Tests

- End-to-end API calls

- Schema validations

- Vector or aggregation queries

- Backup/restore operations

Best Practices for MVUs

To ensure a smooth upgrade, follow these **best practices**:

1. Backup First

Always create a **manual snapshot** of your cluster before beginning the upgrade.

2. Use Cloned Clusters for Testing

Simulate the upgrade in a clone to reduce risk in production environments.

3. Schedule During Low-Traffic Windows

Plan upgrades during **off-peak hours** to minimize impact on customers.

4. Monitor Upgrade Progress Closely

Use CloudWatch, logs, and events to detect anomalies early.

5. Update Drivers and Clients

Ensure your application uses **MongoDB drivers** that support the target engine version.

6. Automate Rollback Strategy

If post-upgrade validation fails, have a plan to **restore from the snapshot** or promote a standby cluster.

7. Validate All Workloads

Perform validation on real workloads, not just unit or synthetic tests.

Troubleshooting Common MVU Issues

✕ Upgrade Fails to Start

Cause: Ongoing backups, snapshots, or unhealthy instance.

Resolution:

- Wait for backups to finish.

- Ensure cluster status is available.

- Restart any failed instances.

✕ Cluster Stuck in "modifying" State

Cause: Insufficient permissions or conflicting operations.

Resolution:

- Ensure IAM role has full docdb:ModifyDBCluster access.

- Cancel other pending operations (e.g., snapshot copy or replica scaling).

✕ Application Errors After Upgrade

Cause: Driver incompatibility or deprecated features.

Resolution:

- Check driver version compatibility.

- Review functional differences in DocumentDB Developer Guide.

- Revert to snapshot if issues persist.

✕ Increased Replica Lag or Performance Degradation

Cause: Indexes or queries not optimized for new engine.

Resolution:

- Review CloudWatch ReplicationLag and query metrics.

- Rebuild indexes or re-tune queries.

- Monitor memory usage and scale instance class if needed.

MVU Limitations and Considerations

- You cannot downgrade once the cluster is upgraded.

- Only certain source versions (3.6, 4.0) are eligible for direct upgrade to 5.0.

- Major version upgrades **are not automatic**—they must be initiated manually.

- Elastic clusters use a different upgrade model (not covered here).

Summary

Engine upgrades in Amazon DocumentDB are critical for accessing new features, performance improvements, and security patches. The **MVU process**, when executed using cloned clusters, pre-upgrade validation, and careful monitoring, can be done with minimal downtime and high confidence.

By adopting the best practices and preparing for potential issues, you can ensure that your DocumentDB clusters remain modern, secure, and aligned with evolving application needs.

Part IX – Real-World Applications and Integrations

Chapter 28: Designing Scalable Document Data Models

Modeling Strategies

Designing scalable data models for Amazon DocumentDB (with MongoDB compatibility) requires a solid understanding of both your application access patterns and the flexibility of the document-oriented paradigm. Unlike traditional relational databases that rely on normalized schemas and table joins, document databases like Amazon DocumentDB embrace denormalization and hierarchical data representation.

Effective data modeling in DocumentDB focuses on optimizing performance, scalability, and developer productivity while aligning closely with how your application reads and writes data.

Understand the Document Model

Amazon DocumentDB stores data in **documents**, which are flexible, schema-less JSON-like structures (BSON). A document typically represents a single entity or object, and it can nest other documents and arrays.

For example:

```
{
  "_id": "12345",
  "userName": "jdoe",
  "email": "jdoe@example.com",
  "orders": [
    { "orderId": "a1", "total": 99.99 },
    { "orderId": "b2", "total": 49.50 }
  ]
}
```

This single document encapsulates a user and their associated orders—perfect for atomic access and updates.

Key Principles of Document Modeling

1. **Model according to access patterns**
   Always design your schema based on **how your application queries and updates data**, not merely how the data is logically related. Optimizing for access patterns avoids costly joins and enables faster reads.

2. **Embed vs. Reference**

   ○ **Embed** data when:

     ■ Data is accessed together.

     ■ The embedded document size is small and bounded.

- Strong ownership exists (parent-child).

  - **Reference** data when:

    - Data is accessed independently.

    - Many-to-many relationships exist.

    - Embedded data could grow unbounded.

3. Example:

   - Embed address inside user if each user has one or two addresses.

   - Reference products from orders if products are reused across many orders.

4. **Denormalize when appropriate**
   It's common to duplicate data to avoid joins. For example, storing product names directly in order documents avoids an extra lookup.

5. **Use arrays for sets of data**
   Arrays are ideal for modeling lists like tags, categories, comments, or order items.

6. **Design for update efficiency**
   Use $set, $push, $pull, and other update operators to modify parts of documents without rewriting the entire object.

7. **Consider the document size limit**
   Amazon DocumentDB supports documents up to
   16 MB. Always design with growth in mind—avoid
   embedding unbounded arrays.

Modeling Common Relationships

One-to-One

Example: User → Profile

Use embedding:

```
{
  "_id": "user1",
  "name": "Alice",
  "profile": {
    "age": 30,
    "bio": "Loves biking."
  }
}
```

One-to-Many

Example: Customer → Orders

- Use embedding if order volume is low and rarely
  changes.

- Use referencing if order volume is large or queried independently.

Referencing Example:

```
{
  "_id": "user1",
  "name": "Alice",
  "orderIds": ["ord1", "ord2"]
}
```

Order documents:

```
{
  "_id": "ord1",
  "userId": "user1",
  "total": 45.00
}
```

Many-to-Many

Example: Students ↔ Courses

Use referencing and model the relationship in one or both collections.

```
{
  "_id": "student1",
  "name": "Jane",
```

```
 "courses": ["c101", "c102"]
}


{
 "_id": "c101",
 "title": "Data Structures",
 "students": ["student1", "student2"]
}
```

Avoid embedding large arrays that could
breach the document size limit.

Index Design for Document Models

Indexes in Amazon DocumentDB help speed up queries,
but they require careful planning:

- Index fields used in frequent queries and filters.

- Use **compound indexes** when your queries filter
  on multiple fields.

- Avoid indexing fields with high cardinality unless
  truly necessary.

- Consider **partial indexes** to optimize for specific
  document subsets.

- Use **TTL indexes** for time-bound data like logs or
  sessions.

Anti-Patterns to Avoid

Poor schema design can severely impact performance, scalability, and maintainability. Avoiding common anti-patterns helps ensure your Amazon DocumentDB deployment remains performant and efficient.

1. Over-Normalization

Description: Excessive normalization that mimics relational schemas.

Why it's bad: Leads to multiple queries or client-side joins, increasing latency and complexity.

Alternative: Embed related data that is read together or frequently accessed.

2. Large Unbounded Arrays

Description: Using arrays that grow indefinitely, such as logging all activity in a user document.

Why it's bad: Risks breaching the 16 MB document size limit, makes updates slower, and causes memory issues.

Alternative: Model logs or items as a separate collection.

3. Over-Embedding

Description: Embedding too much data or deep hierarchies.

Why it's bad:

- Large document sizes impact read/write efficiency.

- Increases network transfer and storage usage.

Alternative: Reference entities if they are large or independently accessed.

---

4. Under-Indexing or Over-Indexing

Under-Indexing: Leads to collection scans and slow queries.

Over-Indexing: Slows down writes and uses excessive memory.

Best Practice: Monitor query patterns using explain() and use CloudWatch metrics to fine-tune indexing.

---

5. Frequent Full Document Updates

Description: Always rewriting the full document even when only one field changes.

Why it's bad: Inefficient use of I/O and increases write latency.

Alternative: Use update operators like $set, $inc, $push.

6. Ignoring Access Patterns

Description: Designing a schema based on data relationships without considering how the application queries the data.

Why it's bad: May result in multiple slow queries or unnecessary reads.

Alternative: Design schemas by starting from application queries and reverse-engineering the structure.

---

7. Misusing Nested Documents

Description: Deep nesting of subdocuments (e.g., 5+ levels).

Why it's bad: Hard to index, query, and maintain. Poor performance with projections and updates.

Alternative: Flatten structures where possible. Use references for depth.

---

8. Using MongoDB-Specific Features Unsupported in DocumentDB

Examples:

- $graphLookup

- $merge

- $out

Why it's bad: Application code may fail or behave inconsistently in Amazon DocumentDB.

Best Practice: Validate your data model and queries against DocumentDB's supported API and feature list.

Summary and Recommendations

Designing scalable document data models in Amazon DocumentDB revolves around three core principles: **access pattern-based modeling**, **document size awareness**, and **performance tuning via indexing**.

Key takeaways:

- Embed when data is accessed together; reference when it's not.

- Avoid large, growing arrays inside documents.

- Monitor and refine index usage.

- Always model with the 16 MB document limit and document lifecycle in mind.

- Leverage update operators for partial writes.

- Use CloudWatch, profiler logs, and query explain plans to continuously optimize.

By adhering to sound modeling strategies and avoiding common pitfalls, your Amazon DocumentDB schema will scale efficiently with your application's growth.

Chapter 29: Real-Time Analytics with Amazon DocumentDB

Using Change Streams

As modern applications demand real-time data pipelines and insights, Amazon DocumentDB offers **Change Streams**, a powerful mechanism to track changes to documents in your collections. By streaming these changes to downstream services like **Amazon Kinesis** or invoking **AWS Lambda**, developers can build responsive, event-driven architectures with minimal effort.

Change streams enable real-time analytics, auditing, alerting, caching, and search indexing without polling the database or relying on batch ETL jobs.

What Are Change Streams?

A **change stream** is a mechanism that allows applications to subscribe to real-time notifications of changes (insert, update, delete, and replace operations) in one or more collections. Amazon DocumentDB exposes change streams using an interface compatible with MongoDB's watch() operation, starting in compatibility version 4.0.

Key Concepts

- Operates at the **collection**, **database**, or **cluster** level.

- Uses an **oplog-like** mechanism to capture document-level changes.

- Allows clients to **resume from a previous position** using resume tokens or timestamps.

- Provides a **stream of change events**, each containing metadata and the affected document fields.

- Designed for **high-throughput, low-latency** change tracking.

Enabling Change Streams

Before you can use change streams in Amazon DocumentDB, you must enable them at the cluster level.

Step-by-Step: Enabling Change Streams

1. **Set changeStreams cluster parameter to enabled**:

    ○ Use the AWS CLI or Management Console.

    ○ Requires modifying the associated **cluster parameter group**.

```
aws docdb modify-db-cluster-parameter-group \
  --db-cluster-parameter-group-name my-parameter-group \
```

```
--parameters
"ParameterName=changeStreams,ParameterValue=enabl
ed,ApplyMethod=immediate"
```

2. **Reboot instances** in the cluster to apply the new parameter.

3. **Modify retention duration** (optional):

   o You can retain change stream data for up to **7 days**.

   o Default is 3 hours.

```
aws docdb modify-db-cluster \
  --db-cluster-identifier my-cluster \
  --change-stream-retention-duration 86400
```

> 💡 **Tip**: Keep the retention window aligned with the resilience needs of your downstream consumers. Longer durations give more flexibility in case of failure or lag.

Change Event Structure

Each event emitted by a change stream includes metadata and document-specific details:

```
{
  "_id": { "data": "<resume_token>" },
  "operationType": "insert",
  "fullDocument": { "name": "Alice", "email":
"alice@example.com" },
  "ns": { "db": "users_db", "coll": "profiles" },
  "documentKey": { "_id": ObjectId("...") }
}
```

Fields Explained:

- operationType: One of insert, update, replace, or delete

- fullDocument: The complete post-image of the document (for inserts/replaces)

- ns: The namespace (database and collection)

- documentKey: Primary key of the changed document

- _id: Resume token used to restart the stream from this event

  🔍 **Note**: To receive fullDocument, ensure that the driver or client explicitly requests it.

Starting a Change Stream

Amazon DocumentDB supports the MongoDB driver's watch() method:

```
const changeStream = db.collection("orders").watch();

changeStream.on("change", (change) => {
  console.log("Change detected:", change);
});
```

Watch Levels

Level	Description
Collection	Tracks changes in a specific collection
Database	Tracks all collections in a database
Cluster	Tracks changes in all databases in the cluster

Resume and Durability

If a consumer crashes or disconnects, it can **resume processing** from the last seen event using:

- **Resume token**: Provided in each change stream event (_id.data)

- **Start timestamp**: Use startAtOperationTime to specify a UTC timestamp

This mechanism allows fault-tolerant ingestion pipelines that can catch up after interruptions.

Example: Resume from token

```
db.collection("orders").watch([], {
  resumeAfter: { data: "<resume_token>" }
});
```

Example: Start from timestamp

```
db.collection("orders").watch([], {
  startAtOperationTime: Timestamp(1679520000, 1)
});
```

Lambda and Kinesis Integration

Amazon DocumentDB change streams can be integrated with **AWS Lambda** and **Amazon Kinesis** for real-time analytics, data movement, or automated workflows.

Using Lambda with Change Streams

Amazon DocumentDB change streams can be **streamed to Lambda functions** to trigger business logic when data changes. This is ideal for:

- Sending alerts or notifications

- Updating cache layers

- Kicking off downstream ETL jobs

- Enriching or transforming data in real-time

Integration Architecture

1. **Enable change streams** on your cluster and collection.

2. **Run a polling service** (e.g., Lambda, ECS, or EC2) to consume changes.

3. **Invoke AWS Lambda** with the change event payload.

⚠ Amazon DocumentDB does not natively emit events to Lambda—you must deploy a **custom connector**.

Lambda Invocation Example (Node.js)

```
exports.handler = async (event) => {
  const change = JSON.parse(event.body);
  console.log("Change event received:", change);

  // Custom logic: e.g., send to SNS, DynamoDB, etc.
};
```

Polling Function Example

You can deploy a small service using Node.js, Python, or Java that:

- Connects to DocumentDB with TLS

- Consumes the change stream

- Batches or streams events to Lambda

Using Amazon Kinesis for Change Event Pipelines

Kinesis provides scalable, durable streaming infrastructure. You can forward DocumentDB change events to a **Kinesis Data Stream** for:

- Real-time dashboards

- Machine learning feature stores

- Event archiving

- Downstream analytics in AWS Glue or Redshift

Integration Steps

1. **Create a Kinesis Data Stream** with suitable shard count.

2. **Run a change stream consumer** that reads from DocumentDB and pushes to Kinesis.

3. Configure **Kinesis Data Firehose**, **AWS Lambda**, or **Kinesis Data Analytics** to process events downstream.

Sample Producer (Python using Boto3)

```python
import boto3
import pymongo
import json

kinesis = boto3.client('kinesis')
client = pymongo.MongoClient('mongodb://...', tls=True)
stream = client.db.collection.watch()

for change in stream:
  kinesis.put_record(
    StreamName='docdb-stream',
    Data=json.dumps(change),
    PartitionKey=change['documentKey']['_id']
  )
```

Best Practices

- Ensure **resume tokens** are persisted in case of restarts.

- Use **shard-aware partition keys** to distribute load in Kinesis.

- Use **compression** and batching to optimize throughput.

Event Processing Patterns

Pattern 1: Lambda-Orchestrated Change Handler

- Poll change stream

- Transform data

- Invoke Lambda

- Lambda enriches and writes to DynamoDB or S3

Pattern 2: Kinesis Analytics

- Change stream → Kinesis

- Kinesis Data Analytics aggregates or joins streams

- Results published to S3 or a dashboard

Pattern 3: Search Index Updater

- Listen to change stream for updates

- Sync affected documents to **Amazon OpenSearch**

- Achieve real-time, searchable indexes

Performance and Scaling Considerations

When using change streams for real-time analytics:

- Use **parallel consumers** if latency is critical.

- Ensure your cluster has sufficient **I/O and memory** resources.

- Monitor **lag** using CloudWatch and custom metrics.

- Avoid large, frequent full document updates.

- Use **projection** to limit fields in change stream payloads.

> **⏱ CloudWatch metrics** like ChangeStreamsLag and ChangeStreamsThroughput can be set up using custom scripts or embedded in consumer logic.

Security Considerations

- Always use **TLS connections** for streaming clients.

- Use **IAM roles** with least privilege when sending data to Kinesis or invoking Lambda.

- Store resume tokens securely in **DynamoDB**, **S3**, or **Parameter Store**.

IAM Policy for Kinesis Write

```
{
  "Effect": "Allow",
  "Action": ["kinesis:PutRecord"],
  "Resource": "arn:aws:kinesis:us-east-
1:123456789012:stream/docdb-stream"
}
```

Monitoring and Observability

To maintain visibility into your change stream pipeline:

- Enable detailed logging in consumer code.

- Log errors and retry on failure.

- Use **CloudWatch Logs Insights** for consumer behavior analytics.

- Set up alarms for:

  - Consumer lag

  - Record drop rates

  - Lambda invocation errors

Summary

Amazon DocumentDB change streams enable real-time analytics and responsive applications by providing a robust mechanism for consuming database change events. With proper integration, you can stream these events to **Lambda**, **Kinesis**, **OpenSearch**, or any custom analytics system.

By leveraging change streams, you can:

- Monitor and react to data changes in real time

- Drive downstream pipelines with minimal latency

- Reduce ETL complexity and improve data freshness

- Build event-driven microservices and workflows

Combined with AWS Lambda and Kinesis, Amazon DocumentDB change streams unlock a powerful event-first architecture, giving developers a foundation for scalable, decoupled, and responsive cloud-native systems.

Chapter 30: Serverless Architectures

Building Event-Driven Apps

API Gateway + Lambda + DocumentDB

Serverless architectures offer the scalability, cost-efficiency, and simplicity that modern applications demand. By combining Amazon API Gateway, AWS Lambda, and Amazon DocumentDB (with MongoDB compatibility), developers can build robust, event-driven applications without managing servers. This chapter guides you through designing and implementing a serverless, event-driven architecture that connects frontend HTTP endpoints to backend DocumentDB data stores using AWS-native tools.

Why Serverless?

Serverless computing enables you to build and run applications and services without thinking about infrastructure. Serverless applications automatically scale, are highly available, and require minimal operational overhead.

Key Benefits:

- **No server management**: You don't provision or manage servers.

- **Automatic scaling**: Each component scales based on demand.

- **Pay-as-you-go**: You only pay for what you use.

- **High availability**: Built-in fault tolerance across AWS services.

Serverless is a natural fit for event-driven workloads, microservices, mobile backends, and APIs that require dynamic data interaction — like fetching or updating documents in Amazon DocumentDB.

Overview of the Architecture

The typical event-driven, serverless application stack using DocumentDB includes:

- **Amazon API Gateway**: Serves as the front door to your application, exposing RESTful endpoints.

- **AWS Lambda**: Contains the business logic that runs in response to API calls.

- **Amazon DocumentDB**: Stores structured, document-based application data.

Architecture Diagram

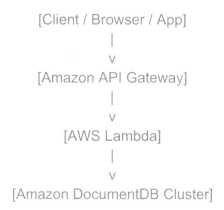

```
[Client / Browser / App]
            |
            v
  [Amazon API Gateway]
            |
            v
     [AWS Lambda]
            |
            v
[Amazon DocumentDB Cluster]
```

Each HTTP request to the API triggers a Lambda function, which connects to Amazon DocumentDB, performs the desired operation (CRUD), and returns a response.

Use Cases for Serverless + DocumentDB

- Real-time user registration and profile management.

- E-commerce order processing and inventory updates.

- Logging and telemetry ingestion.

- Notification systems (e.g., on document insertions).

- Dynamic content delivery (e.g., articles, blogs, feeds).

Designing Event-Driven APIs with Lambda and DocumentDB

Let's break down how to structure each component.

Step 1: Set Up Amazon DocumentDB

Before building the API, ensure a DocumentDB cluster is up and running.

Basic Cluster Setup:

- Choose instance-based or elastic cluster based on scale.

- Enable TLS and IAM authentication if required.

- Create necessary users and roles.

- Open necessary VPC access (e.g., allow Lambda to connect).

  🔐 Ensure your cluster is in a **VPC** and Lambda has proper VPC networking and security group permissions to access DocumentDB.

Step 2: Create the Lambda Function

Lambda functions act as the compute logic that handles incoming API requests. A basic Node.js or Python function can serve as the bridge between API Gateway and DocumentDB.

Required Packages (Node.js Example)

You need the MongoDB driver for AWS Lambda:

```
npm install mongodb
```

Lambda Handler (Node.js Example)

```javascript
const { MongoClient } = require("mongodb");

let cachedClient = null;

exports.handler = async (event) => {
  const uri = process.env.DOCUMENTDB_URI;

  if (!cachedClient) {
    cachedClient = new MongoClient(uri, {
      tls: true,
      tlsCAFile: '/opt/global-bundle.pem', // If using custom CA
      useNewUrlParser: true,
      useUnifiedTopology: true
    });
    await cachedClient.connect();
  }

  const db = cachedClient.db("app_db");
  const users = db.collection("users");
```

```
const body = JSON.parse(event.body);
const result = await users.insertOne({ name: body.name,
email: body.email });

return {
  statusCode: 201,
  body: JSON.stringify({ insertedId: result.insertedId })
 };
};
```

💡 To improve performance, reuse the
connection (cachedClient) across invocations.

Step 3: Configure the Lambda Execution Role

Make sure your Lambda function has:

- Permission to access DocumentDB (via VPC
  configuration).

- Access to Secrets Manager or IAM (if using
  passwordless authentication).

- Basic Lambda execution permissions.

IAM Policy Example

```
{
  "Effect": "Allow",
  "Action": [
    "secretsmanager:GetSecretValue",
```

```
    "logs:CreateLogGroup",
    "logs:CreateLogStream",
    "logs:PutLogEvents"
  ],
  "Resource": "*"
}
```

Step 4: Create and Configure Amazon API Gateway

Amazon API Gateway serves as the public-facing HTTP interface.

Create a REST API

- Define resources like /users

- Define methods: POST, GET, DELETE, etc.

- Integrate each method with the Lambda function.

Enable CORS (Cross-Origin Resource Sharing)

- Add appropriate headers if your frontend is hosted elsewhere.

Deployment Steps

- Deploy the API to a stage (e.g., dev, prod)

- Note the generated invoke URL for use in your frontend

Step 5: Secure the Architecture

Security in serverless architectures is layered:

1. DocumentDB Security

- Enable encryption at rest and in transit.

- Use IAM authentication where possible.

- Restrict access using VPC security groups.

2. Lambda Security

- Use least privilege IAM roles.

- Rotate secrets using AWS Secrets Manager.

- Avoid hardcoding credentials in code.

3. API Gateway Security

- Enable API keys or OAuth via Amazon Cognito.

- Use throttling and rate limiting.

- Enable logging and monitoring with CloudWatch.

Step 6: Monitor and Scale

Monitoring Tools

- **Amazon CloudWatch Logs**: View logs from Lambda functions.

- **Amazon CloudWatch Metrics**: Monitor API Gateway latency and errors.

- **X-Ray**: Trace requests end-to-end across Lambda and API Gateway.

Scaling Behavior

- **Lambda**: Automatically scales with concurrent requests.

- **API Gateway**: Handles thousands of requests per second.

- **DocumentDB**: Add replica instances or scale compute up/down.

Example Use Case: User Registration API

Flow:

1. Frontend sends a POST /users request to API Gateway.

2. API Gateway invokes Lambda with the user data.

3. Lambda validates and inserts the data into DocumentDB.

4. Lambda returns the inserted document ID.

5. Frontend displays success.

Example Payload

```
{
 "name": "Alice",
 "email": "alice@example.com"
}
```

Example Response

```
{
 "insertedId": "6603b9d3c58f7d001dff91d2"
}
```

Best Practices

- **Keep Lambda Packages Small**: Minimize cold start time.

- **Use Environment Variables**: Store connection URIs securely.

- **Reuse Connections**: Persist connections across invocations.

- **Limit Document Size**: Avoid storing large blobs directly.

- **Handle Failures Gracefully**: Retry on transient errors, use dead-letter queues if needed.

Sample Architecture with AWS Services

Component	Service Used
Frontend	Amazon S3 + CloudFront
API Endpoint	Amazon API Gateway
Compute	AWS Lambda
Data Store	Amazon DocumentDB
Secrets	AWS Secrets Manager
Monitoring	Amazon CloudWatch
Tracing	AWS X-Ray

Summary

By combining Amazon API Gateway, AWS Lambda, and Amazon DocumentDB, developers can build scalable, secure, and cost-efficient event-driven applications. This serverless architecture reduces operational burden while enabling rapid development of RESTful APIs backed by a powerful document database.

Whether you are building a user registration system, real-time analytics pipeline, or a mobile backend, this architecture pattern provides a flexible foundation to scale with your application needs.

Chapter 31: Microservices with Amazon DocumentDB

Patterns for Microservice Data Management

As organizations move toward microservices architectures, managing data across loosely coupled, independently deployable services becomes a significant challenge. Amazon DocumentDB (with MongoDB compatibility) is a natural fit for microservices due to its flexible document model, managed infrastructure, and seamless integration with the broader AWS ecosystem.

This chapter explores common microservice data management patterns using Amazon DocumentDB and discusses strategies for managing endpoints and connections in distributed architectures.

Why Amazon DocumentDB for Microservices?

Amazon DocumentDB supports microservices architectures through:

- **Flexible schemas**: Accommodate evolving data models without complex migrations.

- **Independent data stores**: Promote service autonomy and reduce coupling.

- **High availability and scaling**: Each service can independently scale its database workloads.

- **Fast startup with fully managed services**: Eliminate the need to manage MongoDB clusters manually.

- **Built-in security and isolation**: Use IAM and VPCs for secure, scoped access.

Patterns for Microservice Data Management

Microservice data management introduces trade-offs between consistency, availability, performance, and independence. Here are some widely adopted patterns:

Database per Service

Each microservice manages its own dedicated Amazon DocumentDB database or collection. This is the most common pattern and ensures strong service isolation.

Pros:

- Clear data ownership

- Autonomous schema evolution

- Fault isolation between services

Implementation in Amazon DocumentDB:

- Create a dedicated collection or database per service within a cluster.

- Use resource tagging to manage cost and ownership.

```
// Example: "Orders" service using its own collection
db.orders.insertOne({
  orderId: "A001",
  userId: "U001",
  items: [{ productId: "P001", quantity: 2 }],
  status: "pending"
});
```

Shared Database with Logical Separation

Multiple microservices share a single Amazon DocumentDB database but use logically separated collections or namespaces.

Pros:

- Fewer clusters to manage

- Efficient resource utilization

Cons:

- Risk of schema or data ownership overlap

- Requires strict governance

Best practice: Use a naming convention such as service_collection (**e.g.**, user_profiles, inventory_stock) to reduce conflicts.

Saga Pattern for Distributed Transactions

In microservices, distributed transactions are hard to implement due to the lack of atomicity across services. Instead, services coordinate using the **Saga pattern**, a sequence of local transactions with compensation logic.

How DocumentDB helps:

- Use idempotent writes with upsert

- Store saga state and progression documents

- Implement retry and rollback logic using DocumentDB transactions

```
// Begin a transaction for a saga step
session.startTransaction();

try {
  db.inventory.updateOne(
    { productId: "P001", stock: { $gte: 1 } },
    { $inc: { stock: -1 } },
    { session }
  );
```

```
db.orders.insertOne({
  orderId: "A002",
  productId: "P001",
  status: "confirmed"
}, { session });

session.commitTransaction();
} catch (err) {
  session.abortTransaction();
}
```

Event-Carried State Transfer

Instead of querying another service, a microservice can subscribe to domain events and maintain a local copy of needed data.

- Use **Amazon DocumentDB** for storing the local materialized views.

- Use **Amazon EventBridge**, **SNS**, or **Kafka** to deliver events.

Advantages:

- Reduced cross-service dependencies

- Enhanced performance

- Enables offline operation

```
// A listener service updates local state when a user event
is received
db.local_user_cache.updateOne(
  { userId: "U001" },
  { $set: { email: "newemail@example.com" } },
  { upsert: true }
);
```

API Composition and Aggregation

For read operations involving data from multiple services:

- Use a **composite service** or **API gateway** that aggregates results.

- Each service owns its own Amazon DocumentDB data but shares data through APIs.

Avoid direct cross-service reads. Instead, implement backend-for-frontend (BFF) patterns that pull from relevant services and compose the response.

Endpoint and Connection Strategies

Efficient and resilient connection management is essential when many microservices connect concurrently to Amazon DocumentDB.

Connection Types

Amazon DocumentDB provides the following endpoints:

- **Cluster Endpoint**: Connects to the primary instance. Used for read/write operations.

- **Reader Endpoint**: Load balances across replicas for read-only workloads.

- **Instance Endpoint**: Connects directly to a specific instance.

Each service should choose an endpoint based on its workload profile:

Microservice Role	Recommended Endpoint
Write-heavy	Cluster Endpoint
Read-heavy	Reader Endpoint
Debugging/analytics	Instance Endpoint
Balanced R/W workload	Cluster (replicaSet)

Using Replica Set Mode

Connecting in **replica set mode** (using replicaSet=rs0) is recommended to leverage failover, read preferences, and routing.

Benefits:

- Automatic failover handling

- Fine-grained read preference control

- More resilient in dynamic environments

Example connection string:

mongodb://username:password@sample-cluster.cluster-abc123.us-east-1.docdb.amazonaws.com:27017/?replicaSet=rs0&tls=true

---

Read Preference Settings

Amazon DocumentDB supports read preferences to control how reads are routed:

- primary: Read from the primary only

- primaryPreferred: Try primary, fall back to secondary

- secondary: Read from secondary only

- secondaryPreferred: Try secondary, fall back to primary

- nearest: Latency-based routing (less common)

Use secondaryPreferred for read-intensive microservices to reduce load on the primary.

Managing Connection Pools

Each microservice should maintain its own connection pool:

- Use **MongoDB connection pooling** in your driver (Java, Python, Node.js)

- Set maxPoolSize to handle expected concurrency without overwhelming the cluster

- Share a singleton connection within each container or function

Example (Node.js):

```
const { MongoClient } = require('mongodb');
const uri = process.env.DOCDB_URI;
const client = new MongoClient(uri, {
  useNewUrlParser: true,
  useUnifiedTopology: true,
  maxPoolSize: 10
});

await client.connect();
```

VPC and IAM Integration

Amazon DocumentDB is deployed within a **VPC**, allowing services in the same VPC to connect securely.

- Use **security groups** to control which services can access the cluster

- Use **IAM authentication** to avoid storing credentials in code

- Leverage **Secrets Manager** to rotate passwords and manage credentials

---

Handling Failures and Timeouts

Microservices should be fault-tolerant and resilient:

- Set timeouts on connections and queries

- Implement retry logic with exponential backoff

- Monitor health using Amazon CloudWatch metrics (e.g., DatabaseConnections, ReplicaLag)

- Use circuit breakers in service mesh architectures (e.g., AWS App Mesh or Istio)

Summary

Amazon DocumentDB integrates seamlessly with microservice architectures by providing a flexible, scalable, and managed data layer. With patterns such as **database-per-service**, **event-driven state sharing**, and **API**

aggregation, microservices can maintain their autonomy while efficiently interacting with data.

Key Recommendations:

- Isolate data per microservice when possible

- Choose endpoints based on workload (reader for read-heavy services)

- Use replica set mode for resilience

- Implement connection pooling and failure recovery

- Leverage IAM, VPC, and Secrets Manager for secure access

Chapter 32: CI/CD Pipelines and Automation

CloudFormation, CDK, CodePipeline, and Infrastructure as Code

---

Modern software development emphasizes agility, reliability, and repeatability. These principles are brought to life through **Continuous Integration and Continuous Deployment (CI/CD)** and **Infrastructure as Code (IaC)** practices. In the Amazon DocumentDB ecosystem, these practices are crucial for efficiently deploying and managing clusters, instances, parameter groups, and other resources.

This chapter explores how you can automate Amazon DocumentDB deployments using **AWS CloudFormation**, **AWS Cloud Development Kit (CDK)**, and **AWS CodePipeline**. It also outlines key concepts and best practices for managing DocumentDB infrastructure through code.

Introduction to CI/CD for Amazon DocumentDB

CI/CD allows you to:

- Automate testing, validation, and deployment of application and infrastructure code.

- Reduce human error in environment setup.

348

- Maintain version-controlled infrastructure definitions.

- Enable repeatable, consistent deployments across dev, test, and prod environments.

For Amazon DocumentDB, CI/CD and IaC practices apply to:

- Provisioning and modifying clusters and instances

- Managing security settings, parameter groups, and networking

- Automating backup, monitoring, and logging configurations

- Integrating database setup as part of full-stack application deployments

---

Infrastructure as Code (IaC) Concepts

Infrastructure as Code (IaC) is the practice of defining and managing infrastructure using configuration files and code rather than manual processes.

Benefits of IaC for DocumentDB

- **Repeatability**: Deploy identical clusters in multiple environments.

- **Versioning**: Store infrastructure code in Git for auditing and rollback.

- **Automation**: Integrate infrastructure into CI/CD pipelines.

- **Consistency**: Eliminate manual configuration drift.

Common Tools for IaC in AWS

Tool	Description
CloudFormation	Declarative YAML/JSON templates to provision AWS resources
CDK	Type-safe, object-oriented framework (TypeScript, Python, etc.)
Terraform	Popular open-source multi-cloud IaC tool (not covered here)

Using AWS CloudFormation with Amazon DocumentDB

AWS CloudFormation enables you to define Amazon DocumentDB resources using JSON or YAML templates.

Key CloudFormation Resources for DocumentDB

- AWS::DocDB::DBCluster

- AWS::DocDB::DBInstance

- AWS::DocDB::DBClusterParameterGroup

- AWS::DocDB::DBSubnetGroup

- AWS::SecretsManager::Secret (for password storage)

- AWS::IAM::Role (for access control)

Example CloudFormation Template (YAML)

```
Resources:
  MyDocDBCluster:
    Type: AWS::DocDB::DBCluster
    Properties:
      MasterUsername: admin
      MasterUserPassword: !Ref MyDBPassword
      DBClusterIdentifier: my-docdb-cluster
      EngineVersion: "5.0.0"
      VpcSecurityGroupIds:
        - sg-abc123

  MyDBInstance:
    Type: AWS::DocDB::DBInstance
    Properties:
      DBClusterIdentifier: !Ref MyDocDBCluster
      DBInstanceClass: db.r5.large
      AvailabilityZone: us-east-1a
```

Template Deployment

You can deploy the above template using:

```
aws cloudformation deploy \
  --template-file docdb-stack.yaml \
  --stack-name docdb-prod
```

Using AWS CDK for Amazon DocumentDB

AWS CDK is an open-source framework that lets you define infrastructure using programming languages such as TypeScript, Python, Java, and C#.

Why CDK?

- Easier to manage than raw YAML/JSON

- Enables loops, conditions, and code reuse

- Integrates naturally with CI/CD workflows

CDK Construct Example (Python)

```python
from aws_cdk import (
    aws_docdb as docdb,
    aws_ec2 as ec2,
    core
)

class DocDBStack(core.Stack):
    def __init__(self, scope: core.Construct, id: str,
**kwargs):
        super().__init__(scope, id, **kwargs)

        vpc = ec2.Vpc.from_lookup(self, "VPC",
is_default=True)

        cluster = docdb.CfnDBCluster(
```

```
    self, "MyDocDBCluster",
    master_username="admin",
    master_user_password="SecurePass123!",
    db_cluster_identifier="my-docdb-cluster",
    vpc_security_group_ids=[],
    availability_zones=["us-east-1a", "us-east-1b"]
)

docdb.CfnDBInstance(
    self, "MyDocDBInstance",
    db_cluster_identifier=cluster.ref,
    db_instance_class="db.r5.large"
)
```

CDK Deployment

Run:

```
cdk deploy
```

You can also synthesize to view the underlying
CloudFormation:

```
cdk synth
```

Automating with AWS CodePipeline

AWS CodePipeline automates software release
processes. For infrastructure automation, it can be used to:

- Detect changes in a Git repository (e.g., new CloudFormation or CDK code)

- Deploy templates to multiple environments (dev, staging, prod)

- Validate infrastructure via tests or manual approval stages

Sample Pipeline Stages for DocumentDB

1. **Source**: GitHub/CodeCommit repo contains IaC code

2. **Build**: Run cdk synth or package CloudFormation

3. **Approval**: Optional manual checkpoint

4. **Deploy**: Use CloudFormation action to launch/update stack

Example CodePipeline CloudFormation Block

```
Resources:
  MyPipeline:
    Type: AWS::CodePipeline::Pipeline
    Properties:
      Stages:
        - Name: Source
          Actions:
            - Name: SourceAction
              ActionTypeId:
                Category: Source
```

```
          Owner: AWS
          Provider: CodeCommit
          Version: 1
        OutputArtifacts:
          - Name: SourceOutput
   - Name: Deploy
     Actions:
       - Name: DeployStack
         ActionTypeId:
           Category: Deploy
           Owner: AWS
           Provider: CloudFormation
           Version: 1
         InputArtifacts:
           - Name: SourceOutput
         Configuration:
           StackName: DocDBStack
           TemplatePath: SourceOutput::docdb-stack.yaml
```

Best Practices for CI/CD with DocumentDB

1. **Parameterize Secrets**

   ○ Use **AWS Secrets Manager** or **SSM Parameter Store** for passwords.

2. **Modularize Templates**

   ○ Use nested stacks or multiple CDK constructs for better organization.

3. **Use Staging Environments**

- Promote infrastructure changes through dev → test → prod environments.

4. **Set Up Alarms and Monitoring**

   - Include CloudWatch alarms in your stacks to monitor instance health and storage usage.

5. **Enable Change Protection**

   - Set deletion protection or approval gates for production pipelines.

6. **Automate Snapshot Backups**

   - Integrate snapshot creation into CDK or CodeBuild stages before major changes.

7. **Apply Resource Tags**

   - Tag clusters and stacks for billing and tracking (Environment, Team, Application).

Example CI/CD Workflow

Here's what a full CI/CD flow might look like for an Amazon DocumentDB-backed application:

[CodeCommit] → [CodeBuild (CDK Synth)] → [Approval Stage] → [CloudFormation Deploy]

App Code ◄————Infrastructure as Code———— ► |
(Amazon DocumentDB Cluster, Subnet Group, Parameter Group)

- Infrastructure changes are version-controlled with application code.

- Automated pipelines deploy DocumentDB clusters in dev/test before promoting to production.

- Secrets and environment-specific variables are injected securely.

Integrating with Third-Party Tools

While AWS-native tools are powerful, Amazon DocumentDB CI/CD workflows can also integrate with:

- **Terraform** for IaC

- **Jenkins**, **GitLab CI**, or **GitHub Actions** for custom pipelines

- **Ansible** or **Pulumi** for advanced automation

These tools can call AWS APIs, invoke CDK apps, or trigger CloudFormation deployments as part of broader DevOps pipelines.

Monitoring and Rollbacks

After deployment:

- Use **CloudWatch** to monitor cluster metrics like CPU, memory, and replication lag.

- Enable **logging** for auditing and troubleshooting.

- If a deployment fails, use:

    ○ **Stack rollback** (CloudFormation)

    ○ **Manual intervention** (CDK diff and deploy selectively)

    ○ **Snapshot restore** (if major state change)

Summary

Amazon DocumentDB can be seamlessly integrated into modern CI/CD pipelines using AWS infrastructure automation tools. Key takeaways:

- **Infrastructure as Code** is foundational for managing DocumentDB clusters at scale.

- Use **CloudFormation** or **CDK** to define resources and environments declaratively.

- Automate deployments with **CodePipeline**, integrating source control, build, approval, and deployment stages.

- Follow **DevOps best practices** including staging, secrets management, modular templates, and tagging.

- Monitor changes and health post-deployment with AWS-native tools.

With a mature CI/CD strategy, you can ship database-backed features faster and more reliably, all while maintaining consistent environments across your AWS accounts and Regions.

Part X – Enterprise Operations and Strategy

Chapter 33: Cost Management and Usage Insights

Managing costs effectively is critical to operating scalable and performant applications on Amazon DocumentDB. While Amazon DocumentDB is fully managed and abstracts much of the infrastructure complexity, your choices around instance types, I/O usage, and scaling policies significantly influence cost.

This chapter focuses on how to monitor resource consumption — particularly I/O and instance usage — and how to configure intelligent scaling policies to optimize performance without overspending.

Monitoring I/O and Instance Usage

Amazon DocumentDB charges for:

- **Instance usage**: Billed per second (with a 10-minute minimum), based on the instance class and uptime.

- **I/O requests**: Billed per million requests monthly, with each interaction with storage (reads/writes) counting as one request.

Efficient monitoring of these two key components allows you to control costs and improve operational insight.

Monitoring with Amazon CloudWatch

Amazon DocumentDB automatically emits performance metrics to **Amazon CloudWatch**, including:

- Instance-level metrics

- Cluster-level metrics

- Storage and I/O usage

- CPU, memory, and disk activity

These metrics help you track usage patterns, diagnose issues, and identify optimization opportunities.

Key Metrics to Monitor for I/O:

Metric Name	Description
VolumeReadIOPs	Number of read operations from storage per second
VolumeWriteIOPs	Number of write operations to storage per second
VolumeBytesRead	Bytes read from storage
VolumeBytesWritten	Bytes written to storage
ReadLatency	Time taken to perform read operations
WriteLatency	Time taken to perform write operations

Key Metrics to Monitor for Instance Usage:

Metric Name	Description
CPUUtilization	Percentage of CPU used

FreeableMemory	Amount of unused RAM
DatabaseConnections	Active client connections
DiskQueueDepth	Number of pending I/O operations

You can view these metrics in:

- **Amazon CloudWatch Dashboard**

- **Amazon DocumentDB Console** (Metrics tab)

- **AWS CLI or CloudWatch APIs**

Example: Viewing I/O Metrics via CLI

```
aws cloudwatch get-metric-statistics \
  --namespace AWS/DocDB \
  --metric-name VolumeReadIOPs \
  --dimensions Name=DBInstanceIdentifier,Value=my-instance-1 \
  --start-time 2025-03-01T00:00:00Z \
  --end-time 2025-03-02T00:00:00Z \
  --period 3600 \
  --statistics Average
```

Visualizing with CloudWatch Dashboards

- Create a custom dashboard to display instance I/O and CPU trends over time.

- Add alarms to notify you of sudden spikes or thresholds.

- Use **CloudWatch anomaly detection** to flag unexpected deviations.

Using Enhanced Monitoring

For deeper insights, enable **Enhanced Monitoring** to view:

- Operating system metrics in near real-time

- Per-process metrics

- I/O performance at the disk level

Enhanced Monitoring incurs additional charges but provides granular visibility that is essential for diagnosing performance bottlenecks.

Monitoring Tools Summary

Tool	Use Case
CloudWatch Metrics	Basic performance tracking and cost estimation
Enhanced Monitoring	OS-level visibility
Performance Insights	Query-level diagnostics and bottleneck analysis
CloudTrail	Audit API-level actions related to configuration and cost changes

Scaling Policies

Scaling in Amazon DocumentDB involves managing both **compute (instance)** and **storage resources**. Although storage automatically scales in 10 GB increments up to 128 TiB, instance scaling requires proactive management.

Types of Scaling

1. **Vertical Scaling (Scaling Up/Down)**

   - Changing the instance class (e.g., from db.r5.large **to** db.r6g.xlarge)

   - Increases or decreases vCPU and memory

   - Useful when workload characteristics shift significantly

2. **Horizontal Scaling (Read Scaling)**

   - Adding or removing **read replicas**

   - Improves read throughput and fault tolerance

   - Does not affect write throughput (writes go only to the primary)

Manual Scaling

You can scale your cluster manually via:

- **AWS Management Console**
  Navigate to your cluster → Modify → Change instance class or add replicas.

- **AWS CLI**

```
aws docdb modify-db-instance \
  --db-instance-identifier my-instance \
  --db-instance-class db.r6g.large \
  --apply-immediately
```

Manual scaling is suitable for predictable workloads or known usage spikes (e.g., marketing campaigns, end-of-month reporting).

Auto Scaling (Recommended for Read Workloads)

Amazon DocumentDB supports auto scaling for **read replicas** based on CloudWatch metrics. While **compute auto scaling (for writers)** isn't native yet, you can implement **custom auto scaling** using AWS tools like:

- **Amazon CloudWatch Alarms**

- **AWS Lambda**

- **AWS Application Auto Scaling (indirect approach)**

Implementing Custom Auto Scaling (Pattern)

1. Set CloudWatch alarms for replica-related metrics like:

   ○ CPUUtilization

   ○ DatabaseConnections

o ReplicaLag

2. Trigger **AWS Lambda functions** when thresholds are breached:

   o Lambda adds a replica using create-db-instance

   o Or removes a replica using delete-db-instance

Example Scaling Trigger:

```
aws docdb create-db-instance \
  --db-cluster-identifier my-cluster \
  --db-instance-identifier replica-3 \
  --db-instance-class db.r6g.large
```

Scaling Decision Metrics

Metric	Scale Action
High CPU on primary	Consider vertical scaling (larger instance class)
High read latency or connection count	Add read replicas
High replica lag	Use faster instance classes for replicas or scale vertically
Underutilized instances	Consider downsizing to reduce cost

Storage Auto Scaling (Built-In)

Amazon DocumentDB handles storage scaling **automatically**:

366

- Starts at 10 GB

- Scales in 10 GB increments

- Maximum capacity of 128 TiB

- Only charged for space used

No user action is required, but monitoring VolumeBytesUsed and FreeStorageSpace is recommended to avoid unexpected cost jumps.

Cost Optimization Tips

1. **Right-Size Your Instances**

   - Use performance metrics to match instance class to workload.

   - Don't over-provision.

2. **Use Spot Instances for Test Environments**

   - Not natively supported in DocumentDB, but EC2 clients can use spot pricing to reduce test infrastructure costs.

3. **Minimize I/O**

   - Avoid unnecessary reads/writes

- Tune queries and indexes

- Use TTL to remove outdated documents automatically

4. **Snapshot Management**

   - Delete unused manual snapshots

   - Limit retention duration for backups

5. **Monitor Storage Growth**

   - Clean up unused data

   - Avoid loading temporary bulk datasets into production

6. **Schedule Dev/Test Instances**

   - Turn off non-production clusters during off-hours

   - Use scripts to automate instance start/stop cycles

7. **Consolidate Read Workloads**

   - Use read replicas efficiently

   - Route read traffic using reader endpoints with readPreference=secondaryPreferred

Summary

Effective cost management in Amazon DocumentDB starts with **visibility** — using CloudWatch, Enhanced Monitoring, and metrics analysis to understand how your database is used. From there, you can apply scaling policies tailored to your workload:

- **Manual or automated instance scaling** for compute efficiency

- **Read replica optimization** for latency-sensitive applications

- **Storage and I/O monitoring** to reduce unnecessary consumption

By integrating monitoring and scaling into your operational workflows, you not only control costs but also ensure high availability and performance for your applications.

Chapter 34: Auditing and Compliance Use Cases

FedRAMP, HIPAA, PCI, Long-term Retention

Introduction

In modern cloud environments, **compliance** and **auditing** are not just technical concerns—they are critical business requirements. For organizations operating in regulated industries such as healthcare, finance, and government, Amazon DocumentDB provides features that help you meet regulatory frameworks including **FedRAMP**, **HIPAA**, and **PCI DSS**.

Additionally, Amazon DocumentDB offers capabilities for **long-term data retention**, audit logging, and security monitoring that support broader governance, risk, and compliance (GRC) strategies.

This chapter explains how Amazon DocumentDB helps customers address regulatory compliance use cases, implement audit trails, and manage long-term retention of sensitive data.

Compliance Certifications: FedRAMP, HIPAA, and PCI

Amazon DocumentDB operates within the extensive compliance framework of AWS, inheriting many certifications and guarantees that can support your specific compliance requirements.

FedRAMP (Federal Risk and Authorization Management Program)

FedRAMP is a U.S. government-wide program that provides a standardized approach to security assessment, authorization, and continuous monitoring for cloud services.

Amazon DocumentDB supports:

- **FedRAMP Moderate** for standard workloads (available in AWS US East/West regions)

- **FedRAMP High** for sensitive workloads (available in AWS GovCloud (US) regions)

Key FedRAMP capabilities in DocumentDB:

- Data encrypted in transit and at rest

- VPC isolation using Amazon VPC

- IAM-based access control

- Monitoring and auditing with AWS CloudTrail and CloudWatch

- Multi-AZ deployments for high availability

AWS provides a detailed list of in-scope services and compliance documentation via the AWS FedRAMP page.

HIPAA (Health Insurance Portability and Accountability Act)

HIPAA compliance is essential for handling protected health information (PHI). While Amazon DocumentDB is not inherently "HIPAA-certified," AWS enables HIPAA compliance through the **AWS Business Associate Addendum (BAA)**.

DocumentDB HIPAA-aligned features:

- Data encryption using AWS Key Management Service (KMS)

- Network-level security via VPC and security groups

- IAM and role-based access control (RBAC)

- Integration with Secrets Manager for secure credential rotation

- Logging of data access for auditing purposes

To be HIPAA-eligible, DocumentDB must be used in accordance with AWS best practices and under the scope of your signed BAA.

PCI DSS (Payment Card Industry Data Security Standard)

PCI DSS is the security standard for handling cardholder data. While Amazon DocumentDB is not typically used for direct PCI workloads (like storing credit card numbers), it supports PCI-compliant architectures when used appropriately.

PCI-related capabilities include:

- VPC-only network architecture with no public access

- Full encryption at rest and in transit

- Secure access logging with AWS CloudTrail

- Strict IAM policies and Secrets Manager integration

- Monitoring via CloudWatch and third-party SIEM tools

For storing or processing cardholder data, always validate that your usage aligns with AWS's PCI compliance documentation.

Auditing in Amazon DocumentDB

Amazon DocumentDB supports an **auditing feature** that helps track activity in your cluster. Audit logs can be used to:

- Satisfy compliance reporting

- Investigate unusual user behavior

- Track changes to database structure or access permissions

Supported Events for Auditing

Amazon DocumentDB can log the following categories of events:

- **Data definition (DDL)**: e.g., createCollection, dropDatabase, createIndex

- **Authentication events**: logins, failed attempts

- **Authorization failures**: permission denials

- **User management**: createUser, dropUser, role assignments

- **Command execution**: document modifications, reads, queries

You can configure which categories to enable based on your compliance needs.

Enabling Auditing

You can enable auditing via the **cluster parameter group**:

1. Go to **Amazon DocumentDB Console > Parameter Groups**

2. Create or modify a parameter group

3. Set the following parameters:

    o audit_logs: enabled

    o audit_logs_retention: e.g., 168 (hours)

You can also use the AWS CLI:

```
aws docdb modify-db-cluster-parameter-group \
  --db-cluster-parameter-group-name my-docdb-param-group \
  --parameters "ParameterName=audit_logs,ParameterValue=enabled,ApplyMethod=immediate"
```

Changes typically require a cluster reboot.

Accessing Audit Logs

Audit logs are stored in **Amazon CloudWatch Logs**:

- Navigate to **CloudWatch Console** > **Logs**

- Filter by your cluster log group (e.g., /aws/docdb/cluster-name/audit)

- Export logs to **S3** for archiving or integration with SIEM solutions

---

Long-Term Data Retention

Regulations such as **SOX**, **GDPR**, and industry-specific laws may require storing certain types of data for years. Amazon DocumentDB supports long-term retention via two main methods:

1. **Automated Backups** (up to 35 days)

2. **Manual Snapshots** (indefinite retention)

Automated Backups

- Continuous, incremental backups with no performance impact

- Retention period configurable from 1 to 35 days

- Enable point-in-time recovery (PITR) within retention window

- Stored in Amazon S3 with 11 9's durability

Best used for: Operational restore, disaster recovery

Manual Snapshots

- User-initiated at any point in time

- Retained indefinitely until explicitly deleted

- Can be copied across regions

- Can be shared across AWS accounts (with optional encryption)

Best used for: Long-term compliance storage, legal holds, audit snapshots

Backup Encryption

All backups—automated and manual—are encrypted using the same KMS key as the source cluster. Encrypted snapshots can only be restored with appropriate IAM permissions.

Exporting Snapshots for Archival

You can export snapshots to S3 for long-term, low-cost storage:

- Export as BSON or CSV using tools like mongoexport

- Archive using **Amazon S3 Glacier** for compliance-grade retention

---

Use Case Examples

1. Government Agency – FedRAMP Compliance

- Runs DocumentDB clusters in **AWS GovCloud**

- Auditing enabled for all DDL and user management events

- Audit logs streamed to CloudWatch and then exported to secure S3 bucket

- Data retention via snapshots stored in S3 Glacier for 7 years

2. Healthcare SaaS – HIPAA Compliance

- Uses VPC-only access and encrypted volumes

- Secrets managed via **AWS Secrets Manager**

- Tracks data access and user modifications

- Maintains PITR for 30 days and takes monthly manual snapshots

3. FinTech – PCI DSS Compliance

- All endpoints accessed via private subnets and bastion hosts

- IAM policies enforce least privilege for database access

- Nightly audit logs reviewed using AWS Lambda

- Quarterly snapshots retained for regulatory audits

Best Practices for Compliance and Auditing

- **Enable auditing** and log only what is necessary to minimize noise

- **Rotate encryption keys** periodically using KMS

- Use **CloudWatch Alarms** to detect suspicious activity (e.g., failed login attempts)

- Integrate logs with **AWS Security Hub**, **Amazon Detective**, or third-party SIEMs

- Set up **access control policies** to segregate roles (e.g., DB admins vs. auditors)

- **Test your retention and restore strategy** regularly for audit readiness

---

Summary

Amazon DocumentDB provides robust features to support regulatory compliance, from enabling auditing and secure access controls to offering data encryption and retention strategies. Whether you are bound by **FedRAMP**, **HIPAA**, or **PCI**, DocumentDB offers the tooling and integrations necessary to build a compliant architecture.

Through audit logging, encryption, secure networking, and seamless integration with AWS monitoring and governance tools, you can achieve both operational excellence and regulatory compliance in the cloud.

Chapter 35: Hybrid Architectures

As organizations modernize their infrastructure, hybrid architectures have become an essential strategy for combining the **scalability of the cloud** with the **control and legacy investments of on-premises environments**. Amazon DocumentDB supports hybrid deployment models through secure networking configurations that bridge your on-premises data centers and AWS cloud resources. This chapter covers key components of hybrid connectivity— **VPN**, **AWS Direct Connect**, and **hybrid deployment patterns**—enabling you to design secure, resilient, and performant DocumentDB-powered applications in hybrid environments.

VPN, Direct Connect, Hybrid Deployments

Hybrid architectures for Amazon DocumentDB rely on secure network pathways that allow private, low-latency communication between your corporate data center and AWS resources. The two main connectivity options are:

- **VPN (Virtual Private Network)**

- **AWS Direct Connect**

VPN (Virtual Private Network)

Overview

A **VPN connection** allows your on-premises network to communicate with your Amazon VPC using an **encrypted IPsec tunnel** over the public internet. This is the most accessible way to establish hybrid connectivity without investing in dedicated infrastructure.

Key Features

- **Encrypted traffic** across public internet

- **Quick setup** via the AWS Console or CLI

- **Redundancy** via AWS VPN High Availability (HA) endpoints

- Supports **static or dynamic routing**

Common Use Cases

- Initial hybrid connectivity for **testing or dev environments**

- Backup channel to **Direct Connect**

- Secure access for **remote teams or third-party services**

VPN Setup Steps

1. **Create a Virtual Private Gateway (VGW)** in AWS.

2. **Attach the VGW to your VPC** hosting the Amazon DocumentDB cluster.

3. **Configure Customer Gateway (CGW)** to represent your on-prem device.

4. **Create VPN connection**, selecting routing options (BGP or static).

5. **Update route tables** in your VPC to route traffic through the VGW.

Tip: AWS recommends deploying two VPN tunnels for high availability.

Considerations

Pros	Cons
Easy to set up	Performance limited by internet path
Low cost	Latency variability
Works as a backup to Direct Connect	Limited throughput (up to ~1.25 Gbps)

AWS Direct Connect

Overview

AWS Direct Connect provides a **dedicated, private network connection** from your data center to AWS. It bypasses the public internet, delivering **consistent performance**, **lower latency**, and **higher security**.

Key Features

- **Dedicated 1 Gbps to 100 Gbps** connections

- **Consistent network performance**

- Reduced data transfer costs compared to internet-based VPNs

- Optional **Direct Connect Gateway** for multi-region access

Ideal Use Cases

- Production-grade hybrid workloads

- Applications with **high-throughput, low-latency** needs

- **Sensitive data workloads** requiring private links

- **Database replication** or ETL pipelines between on-prem and cloud

Direct Connect Setup Workflow

1. **Create a Direct Connect connection** in the AWS Console.

2. **Set up a Virtual Interface (VIF)** — private for VPC access.

3. Use a **Direct Connect Gateway** if connecting across AWS Regions.

4. **Attach the VIF** to your VPC hosting DocumentDB via a Virtual Private Gateway.

5. **Update your route tables** to allow communication.

   Note: You can use **VPN over Direct Connect** for encryption if needed.

Comparison with VPN

Feature	AWS Direct Connect	VPN
Performance	High (1–100 Gbps)	Medium (~1.25 Gbps max)
Reliability	Very high (dedicated fiber)	Variable (depends on internet)
Security	Private network path	Encrypted over internet
Setup Time	Weeks (physical provisioning)	Minutes to hours
Cost	Higher (port fees + data)	Lower (pay-as-you-go)

Hybrid Deployment Patterns

Hybrid architectures vary based on the placement of workloads, latency requirements, and security policies. Amazon DocumentDB fits into several hybrid patterns effectively.

1. Application On-Premises, DocumentDB in AWS

Use case: Legacy applications access Amazon DocumentDB as the backend via VPN or Direct Connect.

- **Benefits:**

  - Minimal changes to existing applications

- - Leverages cloud scalability without full migration

- **Challenges:**

  - - Latency-sensitive applications may suffer performance issues

- **Best Practices:**

  - - Use **connection pooling** and **caching** to mitigate latency

  - - Prefer **Direct Connect** for production workloads

---

2. Federated Querying and BI Tools

Use case: On-prem analytics or BI tools connect to DocumentDB to generate reports or dashboards.

- **Tools:** Tableau, Power BI, Microsoft Excel via ODBC/JDBC

- **Integration:**

  - - Use **ODBC/JDBC drivers**

  - - Connect via **Direct Connect or VPN**

- **Optimization Tips:**

○ Avoid long-running queries

○ Use **projection and indexes** to reduce result set sizes

---

3. Hybrid Data Ingestion Pipelines

Use case: On-prem systems stream data (logs, telemetry, transactions) to DocumentDB for storage and processing.

- **Integration methods:**

    ○ AWS DMS (Database Migration Service)

    ○ Custom ETL with Lambda or Kinesis Firehose

    ○ Kafka Connect with AWS PrivateLink

- **Security:**

    ○ Use **TLS encryption in transit**

    ○ Prefer IAM roles or VPC endpoints for secure access

---

4. Disaster Recovery and Data Backup

Use case: Amazon DocumentDB serves as a warm or cold standby for an on-premises MongoDB or vice versa.

- **Deployment considerations:**

  - Use **AWS DMS** for ongoing replication

  - Enable **Point-In-Time Recovery** on DocumentDB

- **Backup strategy:**

  - Automate **snapshot exports** to Amazon S3

  - Use **lifecycle policies** for archival compliance

---

5. Edge and IoT Hybrid Models

Use case: Edge devices or factories store data locally but replicate it to DocumentDB in the cloud.

- **Architecture:**

  - Local buffering and processing (Greengrass, IoT Core)

  - Cloud-side DocumentDB for aggregation and analytics

- **Benefits:**

  - Reduced local storage costs

○ Centralized analysis in the cloud

Security and Governance in Hybrid Architectures

Securing hybrid architectures requires careful planning:

- Use **AWS IAM policies** and **VPC security groups** to restrict access.

- Enable **TLS encryption** for all connections.

- Use **Secrets Manager** to rotate credentials securely.

- Monitor access with **CloudTrail** and **CloudWatch Logs**.

- Audit **network paths** for misconfigurations or exposure.

Monitoring Hybrid Connectivity

Key monitoring tools for hybrid environments include:

Tool	Purpose
CloudWatch Metrics	Network throughput, latency, errors
VPC Flow Logs	Audit packet-level traffic
AWS DMS Logs	Check replication status
VPN Tunnel Status	Track uptime and failovers

388

| Direct Connect Health | Port and circuit status |

Summary

Hybrid architectures are a powerful way to transition into the cloud without sacrificing control or legacy infrastructure. Amazon DocumentDB supports a wide range of hybrid use cases by offering secure, scalable, and high-performance connectivity via **VPN and AWS Direct Connect**. By selecting the right connectivity method and deployment strategy, you can build resilient, future-ready hybrid data platforms that take advantage of both cloud-native capabilities and on-premises assets.

Chapter 36: AI/ML with DocumentDB

As AI and machine learning workloads become more prevalent across modern applications, database systems must evolve to support not only structured queries but also **semantic understanding** and **intelligent data retrieval**. Amazon DocumentDB is rapidly adapting to meet this need, offering key integrations with AI/ML platforms such as **Amazon SageMaker** and features like **Vector Search** to support Generative AI and similarity search use cases.

This chapter explores:

- How Amazon DocumentDB integrates with **Amazon SageMaker** for low-code/no-code ML workflows

- How to use **Vector Search and embedding storage** to power semantic search, recommendation engines, and AI-enhanced querying

---

SageMaker Integration

Amazon DocumentDB supports integration with **Amazon SageMaker Canvas**, a no-code environment that allows analysts and developers to build machine learning models without writing code. This integration empowers users to leverage their operational document data in DocumentDB to:

- Build predictive models

- Perform intelligent document classification

- Detect anomalies in datasets

- Extract insights for decision-making

Benefits of Integration

- **No-Code Experience**: Use SageMaker Canvas to connect, prepare, and visualize DocumentDB data.

- **Secure IAM-Based Access**: Controlled via fine-grained AWS Identity and Access Management (IAM) policies.

- **Reusable Models**: ML models built in SageMaker Canvas can be exported and deployed in pipelines or applications.

Prerequisites

Before enabling SageMaker Canvas to connect to Amazon DocumentDB, the following prerequisites must be satisfied:

1. **SageMaker Domain and User Profile**:

    ○ You must configure a SageMaker Domain and at least one user profile for Canvas access.

2. **IAM Permissions**:

   ○ IAM roles must have access to:

     ■ Amazon DocumentDB clusters

     ■ SageMaker services

     ■ Amazon S3 (for temporary storage and data movement)

3. **Amazon DocumentDB Cluster Configuration**:

   ○ The DocumentDB cluster must be accessible from SageMaker, typically in the same VPC or via VPC peering.

   ○ The cluster parameter group must be configured to allow access from SageMaker's security groups.

Step-by-Step Integration

1. **Create a SageMaker Domain** with a user profile that has Canvas enabled.

2. **Create an IAM Role** for the user that grants access to:

   ○ docdb:Connect

   ○ s3:* (for data staging)

o   secretsmanager:GetSecretValue (if
    credentials are stored securely)

3. **Enable SageMaker Canvas** in your SageMaker
   Domain settings.

4. **Connect to DocumentDB**:

   o   In SageMaker Canvas, select **Amazon
       DocumentDB** as a data source.

   o   Provide endpoint, credentials (or secret
       ARN), and database/collection details.

5. **Load and Explore Data**:

   o   Use Canvas UI to explore collections, apply
       filters, and prepare data for training.

6. **Build and Evaluate ML Models**:

   o   Choose a model objective (e.g.,
       classification, forecasting).

   o   Train and visualize model performance.

7. **Export Results or Deploy**:

   o   Save predictions to S3 or integrate into
       operational dashboards and workflows.

Tip: Use SageMaker's built-in Explainability tools to interpret model outputs and feature importance.

Vector Search and Embedding Storage

Amazon DocumentDB now includes **native vector search** capabilities, making it suitable for **semantic search**, **recommendation engines**, and **generative AI** applications.

What is Vector Search?

Vector search allows querying based on **vector similarity** rather than keyword matching. It enables DocumentDB to:

- Search documents by **meaning**, not just exact terms.

- Retrieve nearest neighbors in high-dimensional space.

- Store and index **embeddings** (vector representations of text, images, etc.).

Use Cases

- **Semantic Search**: Query documents based on natural language meaning.

- **Recommendation Engines**: Match users with similar preferences or content.

- **Anomaly Detection**: Identify outliers in high-dimensional data.

- **Image/Text Embedding Matching**: Retrieve similar content using ML-generated vectors.

Workflow Overview

```
                    [ Data Source ]
                          ↓
[ Embedding Model (e.g., SageMaker, Hugging Face, OpenAI) ]
                          ↓
          [ Store Vectors in DocumentDB ]
                          ↓
              [ Create Vector Index ]
                          ↓
          [ Query using $vectorSearch ]
```

Inserting Embeddings

Each document that participates in a vector search must include an array of float values (embedding vector):

```
{
  "_id": "product123",
  "title": "Noise-cancelling headphones",
  "embedding": [0.15, 0.88, 0.01, ..., 0.47]
}
```

Vectors must be **float32 arrays** and can have up to **2048 dimensions**.

> **Note**: You must use an external model (e.g., from SageMaker or Hugging Face) to

generate the embedding vectors before inserting them.

Creating a Vector Index

Use the $vectorSearch index type to enable fast, approximate nearest neighbor searches:

```
db.products.createIndex(
  { embedding: "vector" },
  {
    type: "vectorSearch",
    numDimensions: 768,
    similarity: "cosine" // or "dotProduct", "euclidean"
  }
)
```

- **similarity options**:

    - cosine: Measures angle between vectors

    - dotProduct: Projects vector similarity

    - euclidean: Measures distance

    Tip: Choose the similarity type that matches your embedding model's training objective.

Querying Vectors

Use the $vectorSearch operator to find the most similar vectors:

```
db.products.find({
  $vectorSearch: {
    queryVector: [0.14, 0.85, 0.03, ..., 0.49],
    path: "embedding",
    k: 5
  }
})
```

- queryVector: The vector you're searching with

- path: Field name containing vectors

- k: Number of nearest neighbors to return

Getting Index Definitions

You can inspect the existing vector indexes:

```
db.products.getIndexes()
```

Or retrieve details programmatically:

```
db.runCommand({ listIndexes: "products" })
```

Performance & Best Practices

- **Embedding Size**: Keep vector dimensions under 1024 for optimal performance.

- **Batch Ingestion**: Insert data in batches for better write throughput.

- **Compression**: Vector indexes are stored uncompressed; plan storage accordingly.

- **Index Limit**: You can create **only one vector index per collection**.

- **Memory Optimization**: Choose the right instance class (R6g, R6gd) to handle vector workloads efficiently.

Combined AI/ML Workflows

With SageMaker and Vector Search, you can build end-to-end AI pipelines:

1. Use SageMaker to generate embeddings from unstructured data (e.g., product descriptions).

2. Store documents and embeddings in Amazon DocumentDB.

3. Query using $vectorSearch to find semantically similar items.

4. Feed search results into another ML model or application layer.

Example: A user enters a search like *"best travel headphones"*. The system converts the query to an embedding using a BERT model, then performs $vectorSearch on product descriptions stored in DocumentDB, returning the top 5 closest items.

Summary

Amazon DocumentDB's AI and ML features empower developers to build intelligent, responsive, and scalable applications. With SageMaker integration and native vector search, DocumentDB bridges the gap between operational document stores and modern AI-driven user experiences.

Feature	Benefit
SageMaker Integration	No-code ML model development
Vector Search	Semantic querying over high-dimensional data
Embedding Storage	Native support for float32 arrays
ML Workflows	Unified pipeline from data to inference

Chapter 37: Future Trends and Roadmap

MongoDB Compatibility Roadmap
Innovations in Cloud-Native Document Stores

Introduction

As the demand for scalable, resilient, and developer-friendly NoSQL solutions grows, **Amazon DocumentDB (with MongoDB compatibility)** continues to evolve at the intersection of **MongoDB interoperability** and **cloud-native database architecture**. This chapter explores the **future trends and roadmap** for Amazon DocumentDB, with a particular focus on:

- Its ongoing commitment to **MongoDB compatibility**

- Emerging innovations in **cloud-native document stores**

- Industry trends shaping the next generation of database services

By understanding these developments, architects, developers, and IT leaders can prepare for future-proof data strategies that take full advantage of AWS's capabilities.

MongoDB Compatibility Roadmap

Amazon DocumentDB was purpose-built to provide developers with a **MongoDB-compatible interface** backed by a cloud-native backend designed for high availability, durability, and scalability. Its compatibility roadmap reflects the dual priorities of **feature parity** and **cloud optimization**.

Current Compatibility Levels

Amazon DocumentDB currently supports:

- **MongoDB 3.6**

- **MongoDB 4.0**

- **MongoDB 5.0**

These versions are widely adopted in the MongoDB ecosystem and provide support for:

- ACID transactions

- Aggregation pipelines

- JSON Schema validation

- Change streams

- Role-Based Access Control (RBAC)

Roadmap for Compatibility

Amazon DocumentDB's compatibility roadmap includes the **progressive adoption of future MongoDB features**.

While it doesn't commit to full parity with all MongoDB editions, the goal is to continue enabling:

- **Application portability** without code rewrites

- Seamless **migration from on-prem MongoDB** or self-managed clusters

- Support for **common drivers and client tools**

Future Compatibility Goals

1. **MongoDB 6.x and beyond**:

   - Continuing to evolve parser and query planner support.

   - Enhanced support for expressions, aggregation operators, and pipelines.

2. **Improved Indexing Capabilities**:

   - Expanding support for complex index types such as **wildcard indexes** and **hashed indexes**.

   - Enhanced **text search** and **geo-indexing** features.

3. **Greater API and Command Coverage**:

   - Broader support for administrative and diagnostic commands.

- Continuous expansion of db.adminCommand support set.

Strategic Differences

It's important to note that **Amazon DocumentDB intentionally omits** some MongoDB features—such as **sharded clusters**—in favor of **scalable elastic clusters** and simplified operations.

This design choice is part of the broader AWS strategy to balance **MongoDB compatibility** with **cloud-native efficiency and automation**.

Innovations in Cloud-Native Document Stores

Amazon DocumentDB isn't just replicating MongoDB—it's reinventing document databases for the cloud era. This section explores the architectural and feature-level innovations AWS is pursuing to define the **next generation of document databases**.

---

1. Separation of Compute and Storage

One of Amazon DocumentDB's core architectural innovations is the **decoupling of compute and storage layers**, allowing:

- Independent scaling of resources

- Faster failovers

- Cost efficiency through shared storage

This model removes the traditional constraints of monolithic deployments and enables **horizontal scaling** with minimal overhead.

---

2. Elastic Clusters

With the introduction of **Elastic Clusters**, Amazon DocumentDB now supports:

- **Millions of reads/writes per second**

- **Petabyte-scale document stores**

- Dynamic scaling of compute and storage resources

- Seamless **shard management**, automated by AWS

Features of Elastic Clusters

- Auto-sharding of collections based on **configurable shard keys**

- **Scale-out** read/write throughput

- Built-in **monitoring and balancing**

- Multi-tenant workloads optimized through workload isolation

This feature positions DocumentDB to meet the needs of **enterprise-scale workloads** with minimal administrative effort.

---

3. Native Vector Search

In response to the rise of **AI/ML workloads** and **semantic search applications**, Amazon DocumentDB now includes **native vector search** capabilities:

- Store **high-dimensional vectors** directly within documents

- Create **vector indexes** for similarity search

- Perform **KNN queries** to support recommendation engines and NLP use cases

Use Cases

- Generative AI: Retrieve contextually relevant chunks from embeddings

- Personalization engines: Similar product suggestions

- Fraud detection: Pattern matching in vector space

Amazon DocumentDB's vector search roadmap aligns it closely with modern application needs around **retrieval-augmented generation (RAG)** and intelligent search.

---

4. JSON Schema Validation

Introduced in DocumentDB 5.0, **JSON Schema validation** enables developers to define and enforce document structure, types, and constraints. This feature strengthens **data governance** and aligns NoSQL with the data integrity principles of traditional RDBMS.

Future Enhancements

- Expanded support for JSON Schema Draft 7+ standards

- Schema introspection tools and performance optimizations

- Integration with DevOps workflows for **schema versioning**

---

5. Change Streams and Event-Driven Architecture

Change streams provide **real-time data propagation** for event-driven systems and microservices. The DocumentDB roadmap includes enhancements such as:

- **Granular event filters** for more selective change capture

- **Lambda integration templates** for auto-triggered workflows

- Support for **secondary node change streams**

These advancements position DocumentDB as a key component in **real-time data pipelines**, serving use cases like:

- Live dashboards

- Cache invalidation

- Cross-system replication

---

6. Serverless and Consumption-Based Models (Preview/Future)

As of now, Amazon DocumentDB is provisioned on instance-based or elastic cluster models. However, AWS continues to explore **serverless modes** for DocumentDB, enabling:

- On-demand scaling with **per-request billing**

- Zero-cost idle instances

- Event-based activation (e.g., via API Gateway or Lambda)

Such models promise significant cost optimization for spiky workloads or long-tail services.

---

7. AI-Assisted Query Optimization (Exploratory)

AWS has begun integrating **AI/ML techniques** into query planning and performance insights, aiming for features like:

- **Autonomous index recommendations**

- **Query path prediction** and cost estimation

- ML-based **resource forecasting**

These will be especially powerful for **large, multi-tenant workloads** and **dev environments** lacking dedicated DBAs.

Trends in the Broader NoSQL Ecosystem

While Amazon DocumentDB is a standout in cloud-native document stores, several trends are shaping the entire NoSQL ecosystem:

a. Multi-Model Convergence

Databases are increasingly supporting hybrid models:

- Document + Graph (e.g., Neptune integration)

- Document + Time Series (via TTL and aggregation pipelines)

b. Developer-Centric Tools

Growing demand for:

- **Intuitive SDKs**

- **Visual query builders**

- **Schema visualizers** and IDE plugins

c. Zero-ETL Pipelines

Integration with Amazon services like **S3**, **Kinesis**, and **OpenSearch** is pushing DocumentDB toward **zero-ETL** architectures.

d. Workload-Driven Optimization

Automatic tuning, resource scaling, and cost-based routing will define next-gen NoSQL systems.

Summary

Amazon DocumentDB is evolving beyond MongoDB compatibility into a **cloud-native platform for modern data applications**. Its roadmap reflects AWS's commitment to:

- Preserving **developer familiarity** through MongoDB compatibility

- Innovating with features like **elastic clusters**, **vector search**, and **serverless models**

- Enhancing operational intelligence via **AI-powered diagnostics** and **performance tuning**

By understanding these future trends, organizations can confidently invest in Amazon DocumentDB to support both current workloads and tomorrow's data-driven innovations.

Part XI – Tools, Drivers, and Ecosystem

Chapter 38: Developing with DocumentDB

Programmatic Connections

Developing with Amazon DocumentDB begins with establishing programmatic connections between your applications and the database. Amazon DocumentDB supports **MongoDB drivers**, so you can use familiar libraries in languages like Python, Java, Node.js, C#, and Go to connect to your DocumentDB clusters.

Connection Options

Amazon DocumentDB provides three primary endpoints for connection:

1. **Cluster Endpoint**

   ○ Points to the current **primary instance**.

   ○ Supports **read and write operations**.

   ○ Recommended for replica set connections.

2. **Reader Endpoint**

   ○ Load balances connections across all **replica instances**.

   ○ Supports **read-only** operations.

- Useful for offloading read traffic from the primary.

3. **Instance Endpoint**

   - Connects directly to a **specific instance**.

   - Provides **fine-grained control**, often used for diagnostics or analytics workloads.

⚠️ Production applications should avoid hardcoding instance endpoints due to potential failover and role changes. Always prefer the **cluster endpoint in replica set mode**.

Replica Set Mode Connection

Replica set mode enables high availability, automatic failover, and read scaling.

Sample connection string in MongoDB replica set mode:

mongodb://username:password@my-cluster.cluster-abc123.us-east-1.docdb.amazonaws.com:27017/?replicaSet=rs0

This connection ensures:

- Write operations are routed to the current primary.

- Reads can be distributed based on **read preferences** (primary, secondaryPreferred, etc.).

TLS Support

Amazon DocumentDB supports **TLS encryption by default**. To connect securely:

- Download the appropriate **Amazon Root CA certificate**.

- Append tls=true and tlsCAFile=path/to/cert to your connection string.

Example (Python with PyMongo):

```
from pymongo import MongoClient

client = MongoClient(
    'mongodb://username:password@my-cluster.cluster-abc123.us-east-1.docdb.amazonaws.com:27017/?tls=true&replicaSet=rs0',
    tlsCAFile='/path/to/rds-combined-ca-bundle.pem'
)
```

Connecting from Outside an Amazon VPC

DocumentDB is designed to run within an **Amazon VPC** for network isolation and security. If your application runs outside AWS or in a different VPC:

- Set up a **VPC Peering Connection** or **VPN**.

- Use **Amazon EC2** instances within the same VPC for application hosting.

- Consider **AWS PrivateLink** to expose DocumentDB endpoints securely.

Change Streams and JSON Schema Validation

Amazon DocumentDB supports **change streams** (starting with version 5.0) and **JSON Schema validation**, which enable powerful real-time applications and data integrity enforcement.

Change Streams

Change streams allow applications to listen to changes (inserts, updates, deletes) in collections without polling.

Use Cases

- Real-time dashboards

- Triggering downstream workflows (e.g., AWS Lambda)

- Event-driven architectures

- Auditing and logging

Enabling Change Streams

Before using change streams, enable them on your cluster:

```
aws docdb modify-db-cluster \
  --db-cluster-identifier my-cluster \
  --enable-change-stream
```

Using Change Streams in Python (with PyMongo)

```
with client.db.collection.watch() as stream:
    for change in stream:
        print(change)
```

The change object contains details like:

- _id

- operationType (insert, update, delete)

- fullDocument

- updateDescription

Resuming Change Streams

Amazon DocumentDB supports **resume tokens** to continue from a specific change stream point after interruptions:

```
stream = collection.watch(resume_after=last_seen_token)
```

Start at Operation Time

You can also resume from a precise **timestamp** using startAtOperationTime for deterministic recovery:

```python
from bson.timestamp import Timestamp
stream =
collection.watch(start_at_operation_time=Timestamp(1700
000000, 1))
```

> DocumentDB retains change stream history for **24 hours by default** (configurable).

Integration with AWS Lambda

Amazon DocumentDB integrates with AWS Lambda to enable **serverless processing** of change events.

1. Enable change streams

2. Set up a **stream-to-S3 pipeline** or use custom logic with **Lambda triggers**

3. Handle events in Lambda using a custom parser or event source mapping

---

JSON Schema Validation

JSON Schema validation allows you to **define rules** for what constitutes valid document structure and content in a collection.

Benefits

- Prevents invalid or incomplete data

- Enforces required fields and types

- Simplifies validation logic by pushing it to the database layer

Creating a Collection with Schema

```json
{
  "validator": {
    "$jsonSchema": {
      "bsonType": "object",
      "required": ["name", "email"],
      "properties": {
        "name": {
          "bsonType": "string",
          "description": "must be a string and is required"
        },
        "email": {
          "bsonType": "string",
          "pattern": "^.+@.+$",
          "description": "must be a valid email"
        },
        "age": {
          "bsonType": "int",
          "minimum": 18,
          "description": "must be at least 18"
        }
      }
    }
  }
}
```

Apply it using the createCollection() command in MongoDB shell or driver:

```
db.createCollection("users", {
  validator: { $jsonSchema: { ... } }
});
```

Supported Keywords

Amazon DocumentDB supports core JSON Schema keywords including:

- bsonType

- required

- minimum, maximum

- enum

- pattern

- properties

- items (for arrays)

Use the bypassDocumentValidation option to override validation for specific operations.

Updating Validation Rules

To modify schema validation rules after creation:

```
db.runCommand({
  collMod: "users",
  validator: { $jsonSchema: { ... } }
});
```

Summary and Recommendations

Amazon DocumentDB provides robust tools for modern application development through programmatic access, real-time change detection, and schema validation.

Key recommendations:

- Use **cluster endpoints** in **replica set mode** for resilient and scalable connections.

- Secure connections using **TLS and IAM roles** where possible.

- Use **change streams** for real-time applications and **resume tokens** to ensure continuity.

- Define **JSON Schemas** for critical collections to enforce data quality.

- Combine **change streams** with **AWS Lambda or SQS** for event-driven microservices.

Chapter 39: Connecting BI Tools

Studio 3T, DataGrip

As Amazon DocumentDB continues to gain traction in enterprise environments, business users and data analysts often require access to its data through familiar **business intelligence (BI)** and **database management** tools. These tools enable non-developers to visualize, query, and analyze document-based data.

In this chapter, we'll explore how to connect **Studio 3T** and **DataGrip**, followed by integration strategies for **Tableau** and **Power BI** using JDBC and ODBC drivers.

Connecting with Studio 3T

Studio 3T is a powerful MongoDB-compatible GUI designed for developers and analysts. Since Amazon DocumentDB is compatible with MongoDB APIs, you can use Studio 3T to connect and interact with DocumentDB clusters.

Prerequisites

- Amazon DocumentDB cluster with **TLS enabled**

- Studio 3T version 2022.6 or later (required for Amazon DocumentDB 5.0)

- TLS Certificate: Download the Amazon CA bundle from

  https://truststore.pki.rds.amazonaws.com/global/glo

bal-bundle.pem

Connection Steps

1. **Open Studio 3T** and click **Connect**.

2. Select **New Connection → Amazon DocumentDB**.

3. In the connection dialog:

   - Set the **Server** to your cluster endpoint (e.g., my-cluster.cluster-abc123xyz.us-east-1.docdb.amazonaws.com)

   - Port: 27017

4. Under **Authentication**:

   - Mode: Username / Password

   - User: DocumentDB user

   - Authentication Database: admin

5. In the **SSL tab**:

   - Check **Use SSL**

   - Select **CA Certificate** and provide the path to global-bundle.pem

6. (Optional) Under **Replica Set**, enable and enter: rs0

7. Save and **Test Connection**, then connect.

💡 **Tip**: You can use Studio 3T's **Visual Query Builder** or **Aggregation Pipeline Designer** to construct and export queries.

Connecting with DataGrip

JetBrains DataGrip is a universal database IDE that supports MongoDB-compatible databases via its **MongoDB plugin**.

Prerequisites

- DataGrip 2023.1 or later

- MongoDB driver plugin installed (bundled or via Marketplace)

- Amazon DocumentDB cluster with **TLS and replica set mode**

Connection Procedure

1. Open **DataGrip** and go to **Database > + > Data Source > MongoDB**.

2. In the configuration panel:

- Host: Cluster endpoint (e.g., my-cluster.cluster-abc123xyz.us-east-1.docdb.amazonaws.com)

- Port: 27017

- User & Password: Your DocumentDB credentials

- Authentication Database: admin

3. Enable TLS/SSL:

- Check Use SSL

- Upload the Amazon CA bundle (global-bundle.pem)

4. Configure Replica Set Mode:

- Replica Set Name: rs0

- Add the cluster endpoint in Server Addresses

5. Click Test Connection, then OK to connect.

Features in DataGrip

- Code completion for MongoDB shell commands

- Visual query editor

- Database diagram generation

- Aggregation pipeline builder

JDBC/ODBC for Tableau, Power BI

Business users often prefer BI tools such as **Tableau** or **Power BI** for reporting, dashboards, and self-service analytics. While Amazon DocumentDB does not offer native connectors for these tools, you can use **MongoDB-compatible JDBC/ODBC drivers** to bridge the gap.

JDBC for Tableau and Java-Based Tools

Step 1: Download JDBC Driver

Use a MongoDB-compatible JDBC driver such as:

- **CData JDBC Driver for MongoDB**

- **Progress DataDirect JDBC**

- **Simba JDBC Driver**

Ensure that the driver version supports **MongoDB 4.0 or 5.0**, which aligns with your Amazon DocumentDB cluster version.

Step 2: Configure the Connection

In Tableau Desktop:

1. Open **Tableau Desktop** and choose **Other Databases (JDBC)**.

2. JDBC URL format:

jdbc:mongodb://username:password@my-cluster.cluster-
abc123xyz.us-east-
1.docdb.amazonaws.com:27017/admin?tls=true&replicaSe
t=rs0

3. Upload the global-bundle.pem file if the driver requires TLS trust store configuration.

4. Authenticate and connect.

   🔍 **Note**: Tableau will treat collections as "tables", and queries may require configuration via **Custom SQL** due to document structure variability.

ODBC for Power BI and Excel

Step 1: Install an ODBC Driver

Use a MongoDB-compatible ODBC driver that supports TLS and replica sets:

- **Simba MongoDB ODBC Driver**

- **CData ODBC Driver for MongoDB**

Ensure the driver is installed and configured with 64-bit compatibility for Power BI.

Step 2: Configure the DSN (Windows)

1. Open **ODBC Data Source Administrator** (64-bit).

2. Add a new **System DSN**.

3. Driver: MongoDB ODBC

4. Parameters:

   - **Host**: my-cluster.cluster-abc123xyz.us-east-1.docdb.amazonaws.com

   - **Port**: 27017

   - **Database**: admin

   - **Authentication**: Provide username/password

   - **TLS/SSL**: Enable and specify path to global-bundle.pem

   - **Replica Set**: rs0

5. Test connection and save.

Step 3: Connect from Power BI

1. Open **Power BI Desktop**.

2. Click **Get Data > ODBC**.

3. Select the configured DSN.

4. Choose collections (tables) and import.

Step 4: Transform and Visualize

- Use Power Query to flatten nested structures.

- Apply **column renaming**, **data type conversions**, and **aggregations**.

- Build visualizations on top of the transformed dataset.

Performance Tips for BI Tool Integration

Connecting BI tools to Amazon DocumentDB requires careful attention to query efficiency and document modeling.

Indexing

- Ensure fields used in filters and aggregations are indexed.

- Avoid full scans by analyzing query plans.

Projection

- Use projection queries to limit unnecessary fields.

- This reduces memory usage and network traffic.

Data Modeling

- Flatten documents or design **aggregation views** if documents are deeply nested.

- Consider duplicating or denormalizing data for faster analytics.

Use Views or ETL

- Create **intermediate datasets** by exporting to Amazon S3, Amazon Redshift, or OpenSearch.

- Schedule periodic refreshes if real-time data is not required.

Security Considerations

When connecting external tools to Amazon DocumentDB, maintain strong security practices:

- Use **IAM-authenticated applications** where applicable.

- Always enable **TLS encryption in transit**.

- Store credentials securely (use **Secrets Manager** if scripting connections).

- Restrict **network access** to known IPs or use **VPC endpoints**.

Summary

Amazon DocumentDB integrates with a wide variety of BI tools and database clients through its MongoDB-compatible interfaces. Tools like **Studio 3T** and **DataGrip** allow developers to manage data visually, while **Tableau**, **Power BI**, and other analytics platforms can be connected using JDBC or ODBC drivers.

Key takeaways:

- Studio 3T and DataGrip provide full document query and schema browsing support.

- Use trusted JDBC/ODBC drivers with TLS and replica set compatibility.

- Optimize queries and document models for read performance and BI analysis.

- Follow best practices for secure and efficient connections.

By enabling these integrations, Amazon DocumentDB becomes more accessible to analysts, data scientists, and business stakeholders—unlocking insights from document-based data.

Chapter 40: Limits, Quotas, and Troubleshooting

Quotas, TTL, Index, and Query Limits

Performance Troubleshooting Patterns

Every system has operational boundaries — and understanding these limits is essential for building resilient, performant applications. In Amazon DocumentDB (with MongoDB compatibility), AWS enforces various quotas and limitations across document size, TTL, indexes, query complexity, and instance configurations. Additionally, recognizing and resolving performance bottlenecks is crucial to maintaining a healthy, high-throughput DocumentDB workload.

This chapter dives into the key system limits and shares proven troubleshooting patterns to help you diagnose and resolve common performance issues.

Understanding Quotas and Limits in Amazon DocumentDB

Amazon DocumentDB imposes several predefined limits to protect cluster stability and performance. These include restrictions on document sizes, TTL constraints, indexing behavior, aggregation depth, and cluster resources.

Document and Collection Limits

Limit	Value
Maximum document size	16 MB
Maximum BSON document size	16 MB
Maximum nesting depth	100 levels
Maximum size of a string	16 MB
Maximum number of collections in a DB	100,000
Maximum number of databases	No hard limit (practically constrained by instance size)

📌 Avoid deeply nested documents and excessively large string fields. Consider restructuring data or using referencing patterns to stay within size limits.

Time-to-Live (TTL) Limits

Amazon DocumentDB supports TTL indexes for automatically expiring documents after a specified time.

Key TTL constraints:

- Only one TTL index per collection.

- TTL background thread runs once per minute.

- Deletes are **best-effort** and **not instantaneous**.

- TTL keys must be in ISODate format and contain no array or subdocuments.

```
db.sessions.createIndex({ "expireAt": 1 }, {
expireAfterSeconds: 0 })
```

☐☐ Use TTL for ephemeral data such as sessions,
logs, or tokens. Don't rely on it for real-time
deletions.

Indexing Limits

Indexes enhance query performance but must be
managed within system limits.

Index Limit	Value
Maximum indexes per collection	64
Maximum index key length (single field)	2048 bytes
Compound index max fields	31
Unique indexes	Supported
Multikey indexes (array fields)	Supported
Geospatial indexes	Supported
Text indexes	One per collection (same as MongoDB)

⚠☐ Avoid unnecessary or redundant indexes.
Monitor index usage to detect and drop
unused ones using CloudWatch metrics and
performance profiler logs.

Aggregation Pipeline Limits

Aggregation pipelines allow complex data processing but
have depth and resource constraints.

433

Limit	Value
Pipeline stages per aggregation	100 stages
Document size after each stage	Must not exceed 16 MB
$lookup	Supported (with limitations)
$graphLookup, $facet	Not supported

🎛 Break complex pipelines into multiple stages or redesign to reduce nesting and payload size. Consider pre-processing or caching repeated computation results.

Query Operation Limits

Amazon DocumentDB supports many query operators but also has execution constraints.

Query Constraint	Limit or Behavior
maxTimeMS	Supported (use for query timeouts)
Maximum number of cursors	Dependent on instance memory and workload
$elemMatch within $all	Supported
Maximum sort memory	Limited — avoid sorting large unindexed fields
$natural sort	Supported for default ordering

☐ Always use indexes with large datasets. Sorting without indexes may trigger in-memory processing and throttle your workload.

Performance Troubleshooting Patterns

Even well-architected systems can face performance issues. Amazon DocumentDB provides a variety of tools and metrics to help diagnose and resolve bottlenecks.

Common Symptoms and Diagnoses

1. Slow Queries

Symptoms: Latency spikes, unresponsive API, or long-running queries.

Diagnosis Steps:

- Use explain() to analyze query plans.

- Check for collection scans or missing indexes.

- Monitor QueryExecutionTime CloudWatch metric.

Pattern:

```
db.orders.find({ "status": "shipped" }).explain("executionStats")
```

> ✓ Ensure fields used in filters and sorts are indexed. Use compound indexes where appropriate.

---

2. High CPU or Memory Utilization

Symptoms: Increased latency, request throttling, or instance restarts.

Diagnosis Steps:

- Monitor CloudWatch metrics: CPUUtilization, FreeableMemory.

- Check if the instance class is appropriate for your workload.

- Investigate memory throttling metrics like LowMemNumOperationsThrottled.

  ☐ If sustained high usage is observed, consider scaling up your instance or optimizing queries to reduce memory load.

---

3. Connection Issues

Symptoms: Errors like "connection timed out" or failure to reach DocumentDB.

Diagnosis Steps:

- Validate security groups, VPC routing, and DNS resolution.

- Monitor DatabaseConnections metric.

- Ensure max connections per instance class are not exceeded.

🔧 Use connection pooling and close idle connections promptly. Avoid excessive Lambda concurrency hitting the DB.

---

4. Replica Lag

Symptoms: Stale reads from replicas, delays in data availability.

Diagnosis Steps:

- Check ReplicaLag metric in CloudWatch.

- Ensure write throughput is within sustainable limits.

- Minimize write-heavy workloads without proper scaling.

📎 For latency-sensitive reads, consider using the primary or a well-provisioned replica.

---

5. High I/O Operations

Symptoms: Slow reads/writes, increased latency.

Diagnosis Steps:

- Monitor ReadIOPS and WriteIOPS in CloudWatch.

- Check for inefficient queries fetching large payloads.

- Investigate use of large $in clauses or unbounded scans.

💼 Use projections to limit returned fields. Streamline access patterns for better locality.

---

6. Exceeding Index Limits

Symptoms: Errors during index creation or degraded performance.

Diagnosis Steps:

- List current indexes: db.collection.getIndexes()

- Remove unused indexes.

- Analyze index selectivity using indexStats.

📉 Monitor index effectiveness. Indexes with low selectivity may hurt performance.

Tools for Troubleshooting

Amazon DocumentDB integrates with several tools to assist in diagnosis:

- **CloudWatch Metrics**

  - CPUUtilization, FreeableMemory, ReadIOPS, WriteIOPS, ReplicaLag

  - Use alarms to alert on abnormal values.

- **Performance Insights**

  - Analyze top queries and latency contributors.

  - Identify resource bottlenecks per query.

- **Profiler Logs**

  - Enable Profiler to log slow queries and execution stats.

  - Export logs to Amazon S3 or view directly in the console.

```
db.adminCommand({ setProfilingLevel: 2, slowms: 100 })
```

Pro Tips for Performance Tuning

1. **Use Covered Queries**: Index all fields in the filter and projection.

2. **Shard When Needed**: Use Elastic Clusters for massive-scale workloads.

3. **Avoid Large In-Memory Sorts**: Always sort on indexed fields.

4. **Leverage Query Caching**: Structure frequent queries consistently.

5. **Use Pagination**: Avoid fetching large result sets in a single query.

6. **Use TTL Wisely**: Avoid mass expiry during peak traffic windows.

Summary

Amazon DocumentDB offers robust performance and scale, but understanding its operational boundaries is essential. This chapter provided:

- A comprehensive overview of quotas and limits across documents, queries, indexes, and TTL.

- Proven troubleshooting patterns for diagnosing and resolving performance bottlenecks.

- Techniques and tools like explain(), CloudWatch, and Profiler logs to debug issues.

By following best practices and proactively monitoring your workloads, you can ensure your Amazon DocumentDB applications run efficiently, even at scale.

Appendices

Appendix A: API Reference

DocumentDB API Actions and Parameters

This appendix provides a quick-reference guide to the most common Amazon DocumentDB API actions and their core parameters. Use these to automate management tasks via the AWS CLI, SDKs, or infrastructure-as-code tools.

🔧 Cluster Management

Action	Purpose	Key Parameters
CreateDBCluster	Creates a new cluster	DBClusterIdentifier, Engine=docdb, MasterUsername, MasterUserPassword, VpcSecurityGroupIds, DBSubnetGroupName, BackupRetentionPeriod
DeleteDBCluster	Deletes a cluster	DBClusterIdentifier, SkipFinalSnapshot, FinalDBSnapshotIdentifier
ModifyDBCluster	Updates settings	BackupRetentionPeriod, DBClusterParameterGroupName, EnableCloudwatchLogsExports
DescribeDBClusters	Lists clusters	**Filter by** DBClusterIdentifier, Engine
FailoverDBCluster	Forces a failover	DBClusterIdentifier, **(optional)** TargetDBInstanceIdentifier

---

⬜⬜ Instance Management

Action	Purpose	Key Parameters

442

CreateDBInstance	Adds a node to a cluster	DBInstanceIdentifier, DBInstanceClass, DBClusterIdentifier, Engine=docdb
DeleteDBInstance	Removes a node	DBInstanceIdentifier
ModifyDBInstance	Changes instance settings	DBInstanceClass, PreferredMaintenanceWindow, ApplyImmediately
DescribeDBInstances	Lists instances	Shows role (writer/reader), endpoint, status

🗄 Snapshot & Backup

Action	Purpose	Key Parameters
CreateDBClusterSnapshot	Manual backup	DBClusterSnapshotIdentifier, DBClusterIdentifier
RestoreDBClusterFromSnapshot	Restore from backup	DBClusterIdentifier, SnapshotIdentifier, Engine=docdb
DescribeDBClusterSnapshots	List snapshots	Filter by DBClusterIdentifier, SnapshotType
DeleteDBClusterSnapshot	Remove snapshot	DBClusterSnapshotIdentifier

⚙ Parameter Groups

Action	Purpose	Key Parameters
CreateDBClusterParameterGroup	New param group	DBClusterParameterGroupName, DBParameterGroupFamily, Description
ModifyDBClusterParameterGroup	Change parameters	DBClusterParameterGroupName, Parameters
ResetDBClusterParameterGroup	Reset to default	DBClusterParameterGroupName

DescribeDBClusterParameters	View parameters	Supports filter by Source, ApplyType

Subnet Groups & VPC

Action	Purpose	Key Parameters
CreateDBSubnetGroup	Define subnet group	DBSubnetGroupName, SubnetIds, DBSubnetGroupDescription
ModifyDBSubnetGroup	Update subnets	SubnetIds
DeleteDBSubnetGroup	Remove subnet group	DBSubnetGroupName
DescribeDBSubnetGroups	View subnet groups	—

📣 Events & Logging

Action	Purpose	Key Parameters
CreateEventSubscription	Setup SNS alerts	SubscriptionName, SnsTopicArn, SourceType, EventCategories
EnableCloudwatchLogsExports	Log audit/profiler	ModifyDBCluster → EnableCloudwatchLogsExports=['audit','profiler']
DescribeEvents	View recent events	SourceType, StartTime, EndTime

🏷 Tagging

Action	Purpose	Key Parameters
AddTagsToResource	Tag a resource	ResourceName (ARN), Tags
ListTagsForResource	View tags	ResourceName (ARN)
RemoveTagsFromResource	Delete tags	ResourceName (ARN), TagKeys

🔟 Monitoring & Maintenance

Action	Purpose

DescribePendingMaintenanceActions	Lists scheduled updates
DescribeDBEngineVersions	Lists supported engine versions
DescribeDBClusterParameterGroups	Lists available param groups

Tips

- **All actions support IAM authorization and CloudTrail logging**.

- Use **pagination** with Marker and MaxRecords for Describe* calls.

- Validate **region-specific support** for newer actions or features.

For full syntax, refer to the AWS CLI Reference.

Appendix B: Useful Links and Further Reading

To deepen your understanding of Amazon DocumentDB and the broader AWS ecosystem, it's essential to explore official documentation, community resources, training materials, and relevant tooling. This appendix compiles a curated list of **useful links** and **recommended reading** to help you stay informed, expand your expertise, and troubleshoot effectively.

∞ Official Amazon DocumentDB Documentation

- Amazon DocumentDB Developer Guide (2025)
  Comprehensive reference for all DocumentDB features, configurations, and operational best practices.

- Amazon DocumentDB API Reference
  Detailed descriptions of API operations and parameters.

- AWS CLI Command Reference for Amazon DocumentDB
  Commands for managing DocumentDB via the CLI.

- Amazon DocumentDB Pricing
  Updated cost information for instances, storage, I/O, and backups.

- Amazon DocumentDB Service Limits
  Essential when planning scale-out strategies.

☐ Key Amazon DocumentDB Topics and How-Tos

- Monitoring DocumentDB with CloudWatch
  Understand and configure metrics, dashboards, and alarms.

- Backup and Restore Concepts
  Everything about snapshots, PITR, and recovery.

- Connecting to Amazon DocumentDB
  TLS settings, replica set mode, and networking details.

- Role-Based Access Control (RBAC)
  Control access and permissions at the user and role level.

- Using Change Streams
  Stream data changes for triggers, pipelines, and event-based processing.

☐ Developer Tools and Drivers

- MongoDB Drivers Compatibility Matrix
  Ensure driver support and configuration for

compatibility.

- mongodump & mongorestore Utilities
  Backup and restore tools supported in DocumentDB.

- Studio 3T Setup Guide
  Connect DocumentDB visually with a MongoDB-compatible GUI.

- AWS Cloud9 IDE
  A cloud-based development environment perfect for working with DocumentDB via CLI and SDKs.

🎁 Infrastructure and Automation

- AWS CloudFormation Resource Types
  Reference for DocumentDB-related resources in CloudFormation.

- AWS CDK Documentation
  Build DocumentDB infrastructure using TypeScript, Python, or Java.

- AWS CodePipeline Documentation
  Automate DocumentDB provisioning in CI/CD pipelines.

- Amazon DocumentDB Quick Start (CloudFormation)
  Template to rapidly stand up a DocumentDB

cluster.

📕 Learning Resources

- AWS Skill Builder: DocumentDB Training
  Free AWS training module introducing DocumentDB.

- AWS Database Blog
  Covers new features, use cases, and best practices across all AWS database services.

- YouTube: AWS Online Tech Talks – DocumentDB
  Watch tutorials, walkthroughs, and expert talks.

📖 Advanced Reading

- Amazon Builders' Library: Real-World Reliability
  Insights into how Amazon builds scalable and fault-tolerant systems.

- Amazon DocumentDB Best Practices
  Performance tuning, cost optimization, and security recommendations.

- AWS Well-Architected Framework
  Guidance for designing robust, secure, efficient, and cost-effective systems.

💻 Community and Support

- AWS Forums: Amazon DocumentDB
  Discuss problems and solutions with other users and AWS experts.

- Stack Overflow: amazon-documentdb Tag
  Find solutions and code snippets from the community.

- GitHub Samples for AWS DocumentDB
  Example projects, scripts, and code samples.

- AWS Support Center
  Submit support tickets or use AWS Trusted Advisor for insights.

📘 Release Notes

- Amazon DocumentDB Release Notes
  Track the latest features, changes, and version updates.

Appendix C: Glossary of Key Terms

Term	Definition
Cluster	A container for DocumentDB instances and shared storage.
Replica Set Mode	A connection configuration that emulates MongoDB replica set behavior.
Endpoint	A network address used to connect to DocumentDB—cluster, reader, or instance-specific.
BSON	Binary JSON format used internally to store documents in DocumentDB.
MVCC	Multi-Version Concurrency Control—ensures transaction isolation.
TTL Index	An index type that automatically deletes documents after a set time.
Change Stream	A real-time feed of changes to a collection, useful for event-driven architectures.
CloudWatch	AWS service for monitoring metrics, logs, and setting alarms.
IAM	AWS Identity and Access Management for fine-grained user and service permissions.

www.ingramcontent.com/pod-product-compliance
Lightning Source LLC
LaVergne TN
LVHW051349050326
832903LV00030B/2910